Black expressions

2003 Calendar

Celebrating Black Heritage and Culture

Name *May P. Pete*

Address *P.O. Box 357*

City *Temple Hills* State *Md* Zip *20757*

Telephone *(301) 231-3729*

E-Mail *Wifeyjwamen @yahoo.com*

Written by Adrienne Ingrum
Edited by Lisa Thornbloom
Designed by Barbara Rietschel
Cover painting: *The Drumming* by Nancy Mendes. Copyright © 2002 by Nancy Mendes.

Black Expressions 2005 Calendar is a publication of Black Expressions Book Club, 401 Franklin Avenue, Garden City, NY 11530.

IBSN: 0-7394-2925-6

Printed in the United States of America

BLACK expressions

From the desk of Carol Mackey

Dear Member,

On behalf of Black Expressions Book Club, I'd like to personally thank you for your continued loyalty. Your membership and support of African-American books are greatly appreciated. That's why it gives me tremendous pleasure to present this members-only exclusive desk calendar!

Not only is this beautiful calendar a great place to keep all of your important dates, appointments, names, and numbers, it also celebrates our unique culture and contribution to the arts and humanities, not to mention the written word! You'll be reminded for 365 days of how essential books are in our lives—and how the legacy of reading must be kept alive.

Again, thank you for being a Black Expressions member. Enjoy this terrific book!

Peace and blessings in 2003,

Carol

Carol M. Mackey
Editor-in-Chief

2003 Planner

JANUARY

SUN	MON	TUE	WED	THU	FRI	SAT
			1	2	3	4
5	6	7	8	9	10	11
12	13	14	15	16	17	18
19	20	21	22	23	24	25
26	27	28	29	30	31	

January 22, Wednesday my birthday hopefully my husband will spend a little time and maybe this birthday he might just buy me a gift. And just maybe it will be what I want all he has to do is ask but what can I say. Its important especially when people ask what did your husband give you for your birthday and you say nothing. Makes you go Hmmm. I also took me out to dinner.

FEBRUARY

SUN	MON	TUE	WED	THU	FRI	SAT
						1
2	3	4	5	6	7	8
9	10	11	12	13	14	15
16	17	18	19	20	21	22
23	24	25	26	27	28	

The 25th is the Tuesday for the hearing with workmans Comp. at 2:00 P.M. Hopefully it should go well relax and think when you answer the question relax don't be nervous, answer the best to your knowledge. I don't think I did very well on this because I just could not lie to them. This is so depressing that the stress is a little much I had to deal for the past 12 months with all kind of problems nobody matters

MARCH

SUN	MON	TUE	WED	THU	FRI	SAT
						1
2	3	4	5	6	7	8
9	10	11	12	13	14	15
16	17	18	19	20	21	22
23/30	24/31	25	26	27	28	29

Dr. appt. on the 5th with Dr Byrne same old stuff different day. I'll be happy when this is over so that if they to decide to pay for this surgery I can get it done as soon as possible and be able to go back to work after this ordeal is over. I can't seem to shake this depression my husband is gone most of the time and its so lonely I wish I could travel but it is a little much for me because of this darn hip

2003 Planner

APRIL

SUN	MON	TUE	WED	THU	FRI	SAT
		1	2	3	4	5
6	7	8	9	10	11	12
13	14	15	16	17	18	19
20	21	22	23	24	25	26
27	28	29	30			

Another Dr.'s appt on the 30th same stuff different day. How much more and longer can this go on. I'm tired. All kinds of thoughts are going thru my head now. Strange things keep realing around I'm trying to shake I've been so depressed headaches are happening that this will come to an end but have not heard anything yet spoke w/the attorney says he'll send another letter out. That's all that can be done for now. More times apart what's going to happen

MAY

SUN	MON	TUE	WED	THU	FRI	SAT
				1	2	3
4	5	6	7	8	9	10
11	12	13	14	15	16	17
18	19	20	21	22	23	24
25	26	27	28	29	30	31

Dr appt still the same old stuff Dr. Byrne still says he doesn't understand how come its taken so long says he has another patient who's going through the same thing. My husband is still out there been down to North Carolina a couple of times so he's trying to get where he wants to be but a lot of people are just not into it like he is and I think he losses patience especially when it come to the end of the month everybody watch out!

JUNE

SUN	MON	TUE	WED	THU	FRI	SAT
1	2	3	4	5	6	7
8	9	10	11	12	13	14
15	16	17	18	19	20	21
22	23	24	25	26	27	28
29	30					

My husband has informed me that he plans on taking Sandy down to North Carolina when he goes back. I think my husband has bumped his head he says she needs to get away and have some time to herself because her kids are ~~taking a rest~~ because driving her crazy. I understand what she's saying though because I lost my dad a few years ago and I still cry for him especially when I'm at home by my self I cry and get upset I'm crying though things he doesn't know how I feel he never ask being alone lately has really made me depress. Take me away ... on my head ...

2003 Planner

JULY

SUN	MON	TUE	WED	THU	FRI	SAT
		1	2	3	4	5
6	7	8	9	10	11	12
13	14	15	16	17	18	19
20	21	22	23	24	25	26
27	28	29	30	31		

AUGUST

SUN	MON	TUE	WED	THU	FRI	SAT
					1	2
3	4	5	6	7	8	9
10	11	12	13	14	15	16
17	18	19	20	21	22	23
24/31	25	26	27	28	29	30

SEPTEMBER

SUN	MON	TUE	WED	THU	FRI	SAT
	1	2	3	4	5	6
7	8	9	10	11	12	13
14	15	16	17	18	19	20
21	22	23	24	25	26	27
28	29	30				

2003 Planner

OCTOBER

SUN	MON	TUE	WED	THU	FRI	SAT
			1	2	3	4
5	6	7	8	9	10	11
12	13	14	15	16	17	18
19	20	21	22	23	24	25
26	27	28	29	30	31	

NOVEMBER

SUN	MON	TUE	WED	THU	FRI	SAT
						1
2	3	4	5	6	7	8
9	10	11	12	13	14	15
16	17	18	19	20	21	22
23/30	24	25	26	27	28	29

DECEMBER

SUN	MON	TUE	WED	THU	FRI	SAT
	1	2	3	4	5	6
7	8	9	10	11	12	13
14	15	16	17	18	19	20
21	22	23	24	25	26	27
28	29	30	31			

Birthdays & Anniversaries

JANUARY

FEBRUARY

MARCH

Tisha Thomas

JULY

AUGUST

SEPTEMBER

Will
Bryant May 23rd
Tisha
Tisha 9/16
Christine Birthday 9/28

Birthdays & Anniversaries

APRIL

MAY

JUNE

OCTOBER

Lillian 10/15

NOVEMBER

Hakim 11/25

DECEMBER

DECEMBER 2002 – JANUARY 2003

30 Monday

5TH DAY OF KWANZAA:
   NIA (PURPOSE)

8

9

10

11

12

1

2

3

4

5

6

31 Tuesday

NEW YEAR'S EVE
6TH DAY OF KWANZAA:
   KUUMBA (CREATIVITY)

Odetta born 1930

8

9

10

11

12

1

2

3

4

5

6

1 Wednesday

NEW YEAR'S DAY
7TH DAY OF KWANZAA:
   IMANI (FAITH)

Emancipation Proclamation takes
   effect 1863

8

9

10

11

12

1

2

3

4

5

6

But I am not tragically colored. . . . Even in the helter-skelter skirmish that is my life, I have seen that the world is to the strong regardless of a little pigmentation more or less. No, I do not weep at the world—I am too busy sharpening my oyster knife."

—Zora Neale Hurston
from "How It Feels to Be Colored Me"

The words of this preeminent writer encourage us to approach with relish a new year, still in the dawn of this new millennium. Since Hurston wrote these words denouncing the notion that our African genes are somehow tragic, life for most Americans of African descent has become more and more triumphant. We celebrate our racial heritage with pride.

The oppression—past and continuing—of people of color in America has been, and still is, tragic. But African Americans are triumphant

DECEMBER 30 – JANUARY 5

2 Thursday

Oscar Micheaux born 1884
E. Simms Campbell born 1906
John Hope Franklin born 1915

8
9
10
11
12
1
2
3
4
5
6

3 Friday

Alonzo J. Ransier born 1834
Herbie Nichols born 1919

8
9
10
11
12
1
2
3
4
5
6

4 Saturday

Selena S. Butler born 1872

5 Sunday

Sissieretta Jones born 1869
Alvin Ailey born 1931
Tananarive Due born 1966

survivors who have transformed inhuman hurt into unique cultural expression in every form of human endeavor.

Now that we have more opportunities than ever, an often-overlooked aspect of Hurston's quote takes on an even greater relevance: our busy, overfilled lives are more and more a "helter-skelter skirmish." Her words serve as a caution for us. Rather than resolve to do or not do for 2003, let's simply open life's oysters: taste the salty sweetness and, perhaps, discover pearls. Thanks to a rich African-American heritage, our oyster knives are wonderfully sharp.

The adrinka symbol *Sankofa*, meaning "Go back to fetch it," encouraging us to learn from the past

JANUARY

S	M	T	W	T	F	S
			1	2	3	4
5	6	7	8	9	10	11
12	13	14	15	16	17	18
19	20	21	22	23	24	25
26	27	28	29	30	31	

FEBRUARY

S	M	T	W	T	F	S
						1
2	3	4	5	6	7	8
9	10	11	12	13	14	15
16	17	18	19	20	21	22
23	24	25	26	27	28	

JANUARY 2003

6 Monday

Harry Pace born 1884

8

9

10

11

12

1

2

3

4

5

6

7 Tuesday

Zora Neale Hurston born 1903?
Henry Allen born 1908

8

9

10

11

12

1

2

3

4

5

6

8 Wednesday

Thelma "Butterfly" McQueen born 1911
Shirley Bassey born 1937
Leon Forrest born 1937

8

9

10

11

12

1

2

3

4

5

6

"[Randall] Robinson has not hesitated to put his life and well-being on the line in his effort to involve African Americans in international affairs. His tactics have created an influential political tool in TransAfrica and keep before the public the well-being of Africa and the Caribbean."

—Helen R. Houston
from *Black Heroes* by Jessie Carney Smith

Many heroes, those who do great acts for our community, are not covered in the media, are not even well-known among the vast majority of African Americans. But these heroes keep at their task even if only the cognoscenti recognize their names and the importance of their charge. Often they are not agitators, but rather, highly perceptive individuals who are able to effectively coalesce key powers and resources around a vision that fundamentally changes a core concern in Black America. Sometimes the issues they address—large or small—are viewed as hopeless by many of us.

9 Thursday

Kenny Clarke born 1914

10 Friday

Max Roach born 1925

11 Saturday

8	8
9	9
10	10
11	11
12	12
1	1
2	2
3	3
4	4
5	5
6	6

12 Sunday

Walter Mosley born 1952

As book lovers we can discover these hidden heroes. While the mass media—television, radio, national newspapers—may obscure them, they can often more readily find their way into books. And once published, information about them remains available in libraries and through book-search services, even long after the works have gone out-of-print.

The good news for those of us who love books and understand how essential it is that Black America continue to grow as a reading community, is that as Martin Luther King's birthday approaches, we know he is but one of myriad black leaders. While we salute him, we search out and share with others our many important hidden heroes.

JANUARY

S	M	T	W	T	F	S
			1	2	3	4
5	6	7	8	9	10	11
12	13	14	15	16	17	18
19	20	21	22	23	24	25
26	27	28	29	30	31	

FEBRUARY

S	M	T	W	T	F	S
						1
2	3	4	5	6	7	8
9	10	11	12	13	14	15
16	17	18	19	20	21	22
23	24	25	26	27	28	

JANUARY 2003

13 Monday
Charlotte E. Ray born 1850

8 _____

9 _____

10 _____

11 _____

12 _____

1 _____

2 _____

3 _____

4 _____

5 _____

6 _____

14 Tuesday
Julian Bond born 1940

8 _____

9 _____

10 _____

11 _____

12 _____

1 _____

2 _____

3 _____

4 _____

5 _____

6 _____

15 Wednesday
Martin Luther King, Jr. born 1929
Ernest Gaines born 1933

8 _____

9 _____

10 _____

11 _____

12 _____

1 _____

2 _____

3 _____

4 _____

5 _____

6 _____

---

*S*hallow understanding from people of goodwill is more *frustrating than absolute misunderstanding from people of ill will. Lukewarm acceptance is much more bewildering than outright rejection.*"

— Martin Luther King, Jr.
from his autobiography

King would be 74 years old this week, had an assassin's bullet not cut short his life on April 4, 1968. Had he lived, King would now be a wizened elder among the community of world leaders. Perhaps year-long advance preparations would be under-way across the globe—from such places as Boston, where he went to college, to Norway, where he won the Nobel Prize—to celebrate his 75th birthday on January 15th next year.

Imagine him. Maybe he and Coretta would cel-

JANUARY 13 - 19

16 Thursday

17 Friday

James Earl Jones born 1931
Muhammad Ali born 1942

18 Saturday

Daniel Hale Williams born 1858

16 Thursday times
8
9
10
11
12
1
2
3
4
5
6

17 Friday times
8
9
10
11
12
1
2
3
4
5
6

19 Sunday

John H. Johnson born 1918
Edwidge Danticat born 1969

---

ebrate his special day this year quietly at their modest home in Atlanta, away from the heat of cameras and the noise of broadcasts, and he'd reflect on his life. King would likely remember the faces of the old folks at Atlanta's Ebenezer Baptist, where he and his father had preached. In a flash, he might understand how they felt during the 1950s watching the younger generation—King's generation—completely change the social order. He would perhaps suddenly appreciate their serene joy at long-awaited progress, their wistful regrets at waning body strength that kept them from the front lines of the struggle, and their compelling urge to share with young leaders the wisdom of years that never outdates. He'd certainly survey the dawn of this new century with pride of accomplishment, but most probably he would utter a prayer for deeper understanding for those who continue to block the work that lies ahead.

JANUARY

S	M	T	W	T	F	S
			1	2	3	4
5	6	7	8	9	10	11
12	13	14	15	16	17	18
19	20	21	22	23	24	25
26	27	28	29	30	31	

FEBRUARY

S	M	T	W	T	F	S
						1
2	3	4	5	6	7	8
9	10	11	12	13	14	15
16	17	18	19	20	21	22
23	24	25	26	27	28	

JANUARY 2003

20 Monday
MARTIN LUTHER KING, JR. DAY

8

9

10

11

12

1

2

3

4

5

6

21 Tuesday

8

9

10

11

12

1

2

3

4

5

6

22 Wednesday
J. J. Johnson born 1924

8

9

10

11

12

1

2

3

4

5

6

Driving cars equipped with cameras and tape recorders, they came to the aid of any African American they saw being interrogated by the police on the streets of Richmond, San Francisco, Berkeley, or Oakland. They were visible advocates for black citizens in need. The Panthers served breakfast to children, provided free medical clinics, escorted seniors to and from their homes, and operated a fully accredited elementary school in a predominantly African American part of Oakland."

—Dona L. Irvin
from *Black Heroes* by Jessie Carney Smith

Grass roots, visible advocacy has changed tremendously since the days of the Panthers. While we are a millennium change beyond the "everything is political" rhetoric of the 1960s, the need to reach individuals on the streets and sidewalks remains. We can reach them with books.

As the new year gets underway, many book lovers will ponder what they can do to touch other African Americans beyond their world. Even the most apolitical can get involved through books, and spreading literacy and the love of reading are pretty radical acts. Here are just a few ways each of us can be an organization of one in this effort:

JANUARY 20 - 26

23 Thursday
Amanda Smith born 1837
Derek Walcott born 1930

| 8 |
| 9 |
| 10 |
| 11 |
| 12 |
| 1 |
| 2 |
| 3 |
| 4 |
| 5 |
| 6 |

24 Friday
Arthur Schomburg born 1874

| 8 |
| 9 |
| 10 |
| 11 |
| 12 |
| 1 |
| 2 |
| 3 |
| 4 |
| 5 |
| 6 |

25 Saturday
Gloria Naylor born 1950

26 Sunday
Bessie Coleman born 1893
May Miller born 1899
Angela Davis born 1944

- **Expand your own reading.** Pick up a biography, autobiography, memoir, or other book by or about a contemporary political figure. If this is already a favorite subject of yours, find a new area to explore. Read something different today.
- **Choose twelve books from your already-read shelf and send one each month** to a homeless shelter, prison, Bureau of Child Welfare program, or to someone you know could use the encouragement to read.
- **Volunteer in a literacy program.** You can become a reading tutor and give someone the priceless gift of opening his or her mind to a world of possibilities.

These and other acts can turn ordinary book lovers into reading radicals.

 Akoma ntoaso, the joined or united hearts, a symbol of togetherness and unity in thought and deed

JANUARY

S	M	T	W	T	F	S
			1	2	3	4
5	6	7	8	9	10	11
12	13	14	15	16	17	18
19	20	21	22	23	24	25
26	27	28	29	30	31	

FEBRUARY

S	M	T	W	T	F	S
						1
2	3	4	5	6	7	8
9	10	11	12	13	14	15
16	17	18	19	20	21	22
23	24	25	26	27	28	

JANUARY - FEBRUARY 2003

27 Monday

28 Tuesday
Suzan Johnson Cook born 1957

29 Wednesday
Oprah Winfrey born 1954

27 Monday	28 Tuesday	29 Wednesday
8	8	8
9	9	9
10	10	10
11	11	11
12	12	12
1	1	1
2	2	2
3	3	3
4	4	4
5	5	5
6	6	6

"**In America**, hope is raised by the ideal of its glorious letter and crushed all at once by the letter's cynical disregard. . . .
If only for a moment I could look backwards from the future. From a vantage point well beyond the time left to me. When America is formed of a new and darker majority. When the unseen are at last centered on the masthead."

—Randall Robinson
from *The Reckoning: What Blacks Owe to Each Other*

JANUARY 27 - FEBRUARY 2

30 Thursday

Roy Eldridge born 1911

| 8 |
| 9 |
| 10 |
| 11 |
| 12 |
| 1 |
| 2 |
| 3 |
| 4 |
| 5 |
| 6 |

31 Friday

Jackie Robinson born 1919
Benjamin L. Hooks born 1925

| 8 |
| 9 |
| 10 |
| 11 |
| 12 |
| 1 |
| 2 |
| 3 |
| 4 |
| 5 |
| 6 |

1 Saturday

BLACK HISTORY MONTH BEGINS
FREEDOM DAY
James P. Johnson born 1894
Langston Hughes born 1902

2 Sunday

Sonny Stitt born 1924

Whether the cup of political power for African Americans is half full or half empty depends on one's perspective. We can use the upcoming observance of Black History Month as an occasion to seek out commentators who take the long view, the historical one. And the long view can be summed up in one word: *progress*.

While it is the responsibility of political commentators to focus attention on the concerns of the day, even their finest assessments of the issues can easily overwhelm us if the problems, needs, losses, and inequities of the moment overshadow the gains of the past. Without highlighting the progress made over decades, scores, and centuries, such commentary can lead to a chronic pessimism. The well-intentioned who chronicle the negative in Black America, believing this will prompt efforts toward change, often instead sow seeds of apathy and promote nihilism.

Heralds of victory inspire hope and it is hope that prompts action. In the coming month, let's listen well to those heralding victory.

JANUARY

S	M	T	W	T	F	S
			1	2	3	4
5	6	7	8	9	10	11
12	13	14	15	16	17	18
19	20	21	22	23	24	25
26	27	28	29	30	31	

FEBRUARY

S	M	T	W	T	F	S
						1
2	3	4	5	6	7	8
9	10	11	12	13	14	15
16	17	18	19	20	21	22
23	24	25	26	27	28	

FEBRUARY 2003

3 Monday
15TH Amendment ratified 1870

8

9

10

11

12

1

2

3

4

5

6

4 Tuesday
Rosa Parks born 1913

8

9

10

11

12

1

2

3

4

5

6

5 Wednesday
Hank Aaron born 1934

8

9 *30 A.M. Dr. Payne*

10

11

12

1

2

3

4

5

6

"The Negro girl who goes to college hardly wants to return to her mother if she is a washerwoman, but this girl should come back with sufficient knowledge of physics and chemistry and business administration to use her mother's work as a nucleus for a modern steam laundry."

—Carter G. Woodson
from *The Mis-Education of the Negro*

FEBRUARY 3 - 9

6 Thursday

Anne Spencer born 1882
Melvin Tolson born 1898
Bob Marley born 1945
Natalie Cole born 1950

8

9

10

11

12

1

2

3

4

5

6

7 Friday

Frederick Douglass born 1817?
Eubie Blake born 1883

8

9

10

11

12

1

2

3

4

5

6

8 Saturday

Harry S. McAlpin becomes first black
reporter to attend a White House
press conference 1944

9 Sunday

Alice Walker born 1944

The founder of what began in 1926 as Negro History Week, and has since grown into Black History Month, Carter G. Woodson captured the ultimate purpose of history—memory as a measure.

Far from the dry regurgitation of events and dates, or research solely for the sake of uncovering the past, the exploration of black history is the art of examining the past in order to create a yardstick by which to measure, to assess, the present and the future.

The daughter of a washerwoman who establishes a steam laundry makes a huge leap in progress, but only by knowing her mother's story—the daughter's history—can her success be recognized. Without the history, the daughter's achievement is, instead, just another laundry.

Black History Month is, as Woodson's quote so aptly states, a time to "come back." Without taking time each year to come back to our story as people of African descent, we can forget to measure our progress and thus become cynical; we may grow nearsighted to our victories and fail to be encouraged by their magnitude; and we might despair at our challenges for the future, believing our battle has just begun, rather than knowing it is almost won.

FEBRUARY						
S	M	T	W	T	F	S
						1
2	3	4	5	6	7	8
9	10	11	12	13	14	15
16	17	18	19	20	21	22
23	24	25	26	27	28	

MARCH						
S	M	T	W	T	F	S
						1
2	3	4	5	6	7	8
9	10	11	12	13	14	15
16	17	18	19	20	21	22
23/30 24/31	25	26	27	28	29	

FEBRUARY 2003

10 Monday

Leontyne Price born 1927
Robert Flack born 1939

8 _____
9 _____
10 _____
11 _____
12 _____
1:30 p.m. Kaiser
2 _____
3 _____
4 _____
5 _____
6 _____

11 Tuesday

Nelson Mandela released after 27 years
in prison 1990

8 _____
9 _____
10 _____
11 _____
12 _____
1 _____
2 _____
3 _____
4 _____
5 _____
6 _____

12 Wednesday

Abraham Lincoln born 1809
Fannie Barrier Williams born 1855
NAACP founded 1909

8 _____
9 _____
10 _____
11 _____
12 _____
1 _____
2 _____
3 _____
4 _____
5 _____
6 _____

"a lover whose love was often deliberately misunderstood but who will live in the sun and the rains . . . and who like Emmett Till and Malcolm X will be remembered by his people for the great man he could have become and most especially for the beautiful boy that he was"

—Nikki Giovanni,
referring to Tupac Shakur,
from *Love Poems*

This is a great time to reread or give as a gift Giovanni's book of poetry on love. It takes a great poet to help us see as lovers, figures others have cast as tragic. Emmett Till, Malcolm X, and Tupac Shakur, each in their own generation, were true lovers. Giovanni shows us that Emmett, who was brutally lynched at 14; Malcolm, who didn't live to see his 40th birthday; and Tupac, killed at 25, all lived to love and were loved.

There are precious few purely romantic love poems in the African-American literary canon. The social and political struggle has, by necessity, occupied the vast

FEBRUARY 10 - 16

13 Thursday
Emmett J. Scott born 1873

8

9

10

11

12

1

2

3

4

5

6

14 Friday
VALENTINE'S DAY
Richard Allen born 1760
Gregory Hines born 1946

8

9

10

11

12

1

2

3

4

5

6

15 Saturday

16 Sunday
Saint Claire Cecil Bourne born 1943
LeVar Burton born 1957

majority of the attention of our writers. Those same issues have often robbed our forebears of the luxury of story-book romance.

Elizabeth Barrett Browning penned what is probably the most well-known romantic love sonnet, by beginning with the question, "How do I love thee?" The answer for Africans in America has been, as Giovanni says, deliberately misunderstood. **We have loved in the pain of oppression and been loved bravely with a determination to overcome.** Unromantic, but indeed love.

As we celebrate Valentine's Day, Giovanni can inspire us to learn what love is. The history of our survival is our love story.

FEBRUARY

S	M	T	W	T	F	S
						1
2	3	4	5	6	7	8
9	10	11	12	13	14	15
16	17	18	19	20	21	22
23	24	25	26	27	28	

MARCH

S	M	T	W	T	F	S
						1
2	3	4	5	6	7	8
9	10	11	12	13	14	15
16	17	18	19	20	21	22
23/30	24/31	25	26	27	28	29

FEBRUARY 2003

17 Monday

PRESIDENTS' DAY
Mary Frances Berry born 1938
Huey P. Newton born 1942
Michael Jordan born 1963

8

9

10

11

12

1

2

3

4

5

6

18 Tuesday

Toni Morrison born 1931
Audre Lorde born 1934
Bebe Moore Campbell born 1950

8

9

10

11

12

1

2

3

4

5

6

19 Wednesday

Lugenia Burns Hope born 1871
Smokey Robinson born 1940

8

9

10

11

12

1

2

3

4

5

6

"Five months after the *Brown* v. *Board of Education* decision . . . leaders of the National Urban League (NUL) arrived at its annual conference in September armed. . . . word was spreading through its network in the media to affirm its 'determination to remove the blight and stain of segregation from our national life.' Behind the Supreme Court decision lay no new revelations, said the NUL. 'Segregation has not suddenly become wrong. It has always been wrong.' "

—Janus Adams
from *Freedom Days: 365 Inspired Moments in Civil Rights History*

No recognition of Black History Month would be complete without remembering the role social organizations have played in the progress of African Americans in every sphere. While the NAACP organized the plaintiffs and brought the historic suit that began the process of ending educational segregation—a process that has yet to be completed today—many other organizations rallied to make the decision felt far beyond the chambers of the court.

FEBRUARY 17 - 23

20 Thursday

Sidney Poitier born 1927
Nancy Wilson born 1937

8
9
10
11
12
1
2
3
4
5
6

21 Friday

Tadd Dameron born 1917
Barbara Jordan born 1936

8
9
10
11
12
1
2
3
4
5
6

22 Saturday

James Reese Europe born 1881
Horace Pippin born 1888
Ishmael Reed born 1938

23 Sunday

W.E.B. Du Bois born 1868
Claude Brown born 1927
Haki R. Madhubuti born 1942

Black social organizations have not only been the greatest breeding ground for black leaders, after, of course, the church and historically black colleges and universities, they have also been an important source of self-determined critical analysis, policy development, and social strategy. Without these vibrant organizations on the cutting edge of efforts in behalf of black interests, those interests would hardly be served. Recognizing their essential contribution to our history means continuing to contribute to them, with time and resources.

Akoben, the war horn, summoning us to
collective action, readiness, and voluntarism

FEBRUARY						
S	M	T	W	T	F	S
						1
2	3	4	5	6	7	8
9	10	11	12	13	14	15
16	17	18	19	20	21	22
23	24	25	26	27	28	

MARCH						
S	M	T	W	T	F	S
						1
2	3	4	5	6	7	8
9	10	11	12	13	14	15
16	17	18	19	20	21	22
23/30	24/31	25	26	27	28	29

FEBRUARY – MARCH 2003

24 Monday
Daniel A. Payne born 1811

25 Tuesday

26 Wednesday
Antoine "Fats" Domino born 1928

24 Monday	25 Tuesday	26 Wednesday
8	8	8:45 A.M. Dr. Byrne
9	9	9
10	10	10
11	11	11
12	12	12
1	1	1
2	2 appt w/ W. Comp	2
3	3	3
4	4	4
5	5	5
6	6	6

"His extraordinary success has revolutionized the sport and radically changed the attitudes of black people toward golf. In both senses, this great athlete is a cultural icon of the first order, a young man, in reporter Jim McCabe's words, 'Whose genius brought the game as close to the edge of perfection as ever witnessed.' "

—Henry Louis Gates, Jr. and Cornel West
from *The African-American Century*

This quotation is, of course, referring to Tiger Woods. As this year's Black History Month comes to a close, we want to remember that African-American history is always in the making. The world focuses its lens on the subject once a year during the shortest month of the calendar, but African-descended individuals make history by the second, in the most unexpected places. Fortunately, we can celebrate each breakthrough as it occurs and take each one as an opportunity to reflect on our history and its meaning.

Woods's history-making on the greens, com-

FEBRUARY 24 - MARCH 2

27 Thursday

Angelina Weld Grimké born 1880
Mabel Keaton Staupers born 1890
Marian Anderson born 1897?
Charlayne Hunter-Gault born 1942

8

9

10

11

12

1

2

3

4

5

6

28 Friday

Augusta Savage born February 29, 1892

8

9

10

11

12

1

2

3

4

5

6

1 Saturday

Blanche K. Bruce born 1841
Ralph Ellison born 1914
Harry Belafonte born 1927

2 Sunday

Howard University established 1867

bined with his remarks regarding his mixed ancestry (he has referred to himself as "Cablinasian," paying homage to his Caucasian, African, Native American, and Asian ancestors), raises an interesting issue regarding what we embrace as "black history." The historic achievements of those who identify themselves as mixed race tend to be included automatically in the canon of African-American history based on the obvious—skin color and African-ness of features. The very term "mixed race" was laughably devoid of meaning until this generation because any African blood in one's veins destined one to oppression and exclusion before historic black figures fought down such evils. But, thanks to them, the option may exist in the future either to proclaim oneself a maker of black history, or to choose to deed one's accomplishments to another month, one set aside, perhaps, to observe mixed-race history.

Those of us who cherish the celebration of black history know that pride in our ancestry is ultimately what the salute is all about.

MARCH						
S	M	T	W	T	F	S
						1
2	3	4	5	6	7	8
9	10	11	12	13	14	15
16	17	18	19	20	21	22
23/30	24/31	25	26	27	28	29

APRIL						
S	M	T	W	T	F	S
		1	2	3	4	5
6	7	8	9	10	11	12
13	14	15	16	17	18	19
20	21	22	23	24	25	26
27	28	29	30			

MARCH 2003

3 Monday
Jackie Joyner-Kersee born 1962

8

9

10

11

12

1

2

3

4

5

6

4 Tuesday
MARDI GRAS
Miriam Makeba born 1932

8

9

10

11

12

1

2

3

4

5

6

5 Wednesday
ASH WEDNESDAY
CRISPUS ATTUCKS DAY
Charles Fuller born 1939

8

9

10 :30 a.m. 10:35 Dr. Byrd

11

12

1

2

3

4

5

6

"**Christ is my inspiration, prayer is my work, and service is my contribution. I have learned to erase . . . error and replace it with truth; erase fear and replace it with love. My salvation is my most precious possession. Christ has brought joy, peace, and unending blessing into my life.**"

—Dr. Ruth Powell Maness
from *Sister Strength*, compiled by Rev. Dr. Suzan Johnson Cook

MARCH 3 - 9

6 Thursday

Wes Montgomery born 1925?
Mary Wilson born 1944

8 _____
9 _____
10 _____
11 _____
12 _____
1 _____
2 _____
3 _____
4 _____
5 _____
6 _____

7 Friday

Bloody Sunday 1965

8 _____
9 _____
10 _____
11 _____
12 _____
1 _____
2 _____
3 _____
4 _____
5 _____
6 _____

8 Saturday

Louise Beavers born 1902

9 Sunday

Ornette Coleman born 1930

Spirituality is "in" these days. It's popular to profess to be "spiritual." But being a woman of faith is to being a spiritual woman as gold is to metal. There are many metals, but only one is gold. When one wins the gold, has a golden opportunity, or is described as good as gold, we understand what is meant. Gold means the best.

Women of faith are at their spiritual best. They have transcended being, with its activities of knowing, doing, and feeling, and live on a level of simply believing.

The vast majority of African Americans identify themselves as Christians, but women of faith of *all* faiths are radical believers. They are our gold. They are inspired by the God in whom they believe. They do the difficult, behind-the-scenes work of prayer. They serve as a gift to others.

As we observe Women's History Month, let us be mindful that the most exceptional of spiritual women—those unheralded women of faith—are right now creating a golden history.

MARCH						
S	M	T	W	T	F	S
						1
2	3	4	5	6	7	8
9	10	11	12	13	14	15
16	17	18	19	20	21	22
23/30	24/31	25	26	27	28	29

APRIL						
S	M	T	W	T	F	S
		1	2	3	4	5
6	7	8	9	10	11	12
13	14	15	16	17	18	19
20	21	22	23	24	25	26
27	28	29	30			

MARCH 2003

10 Monday

Hallie Quinn Brown born 1850?

8

9

10

11

12

1

2

3

4

5

6

11 Tuesday

Ralph Abernathy born 1926
Bobby McFerrin born 1950

8

9

10

11

12

1

2

3

4

5

6

12 Wednesday

Andrew Young born 1932
Virginia Hamilton born 1936
Randall Kenan born 1963

8

9

10

11

12

1

2

3

4

5

6

"While preparing for a documentary film on the black theater movement, Woodie King Jr. found that more than forty of the sixty playwrights interviewed professed to being influenced or aided, or both, by Lorraine Hansberry and her work, a tribute earning her a place in the firmament of classic American drama."

—from *The Norton Anthology of African American Literature*
Henry Louis Gates, Jr. and Nellie Y. McKay, General Editors

MARCH 10 - 16

13 Thursday

14 Friday
Quincy Jones born 1933

15 Saturday
Cecil Taylor born 1933
Ben Okri born 1959

13 Thursday

8

9

10

11

12

1

2

3

4

5

6

14 Friday

8

9

10

11

12

1

2

3

4

5

6

16 Sunday

BLACK PRESS DAY
Freedom's Journal first published 1827

The story of Africans in America is an exquisite drama. Women playwrights who have captured slices of it and portrayed it beautifully on stage deserve our applause as we observe Women's History Month.

Black theater is undergoing a wonderful resurgence, as more and more gifted African-American writers produce plays. Yet at the same time it is struggling to survive as "black boxes"—small theaters—close, especially those outside of New York City and a few other major urban centers with large black populations.

But book lovers can do much to celebrate black women playwrights. Reading groups can choose one of the excellent published plays by major writers for the stage, with Hansberry atop the list, as their next selection. The entire group can also support black theater by seeking out local, even embryonic, theater companies and purchasing tickets for an upcoming performance. Should there be no black theater in the area, invite black actors from local universities or community colleges to do a reading of the group's selected play after it has been discussed. Discover how much deeper your appreciation of the work will be.

MARCH						
S	M	T	W	T	F	S
						1
2	3	4	5	6	7	8
9	10	11	12	13	14	15
16	17	18	19	20	21	22
23/30 24/31	25	26	27	28	29	

APRIL						
S	M	T	W	T	F	S
		1	2	3	4	5
6	7	8	9	10	11	12
13	14	15	16	17	18	19
20	21	22	23	24	25	26
27	28	29	30			

MARCH 2003

17 Monday
ST. PATRICK'S DAY
Bayard Rustin born 1910
Nat "King" Cole born 1919
Myrlie Evers-Williams born 1933

8

9

10

11

12

1

2

3

4

5

6

18 Tuesday
Charley Pride born 1938
Wilson Pickett born 1941
Kathleen Conwell born 1942

8

9

10

11

12

1

2

3

4

5

6

19 Wednesday
Nancy Elizabeth Prophet born 1890

8

9

10

11

12

1

2

3

4

5

6

"It was a time when it wasn't fashionable for women to become athletes, and my life was wrapped up in sports. I was good at three things: running, jumping, and fighting."

—Alice Coachman
from *Powerful Black Women*
by Jessie Carney Smith

Nothing is more fashionable in these times than women with muscle. As winter turns to spring, many will begin to think about getting out of the gym and working in the great outdoors. For those who never made it to the gym, the lure of spring can break sedentary habits. It's fitting that the first day of spring falls during the month in which we celebrate women's history. It's a convenient conjunction to remind us of our debt to women athletes in making the world safe for women and girls to run, jump, and box.

Let's not take for granted those who laid the groundwork for contemporary acceptance of

MARCH 17 - 23

20 Thursday
VERNAL EQUINOX
Spike Lee born 1957

21 Friday
Selma Civil Rights March begins 1965

22 Saturday
Houston A. Baker, Jr. born 1943

	20 Thursday	21 Friday
8		
9		
10		
11		
12		
1		
2		
3		
4		
5		
6		

23 Sunday

women athletes and the widespread encouragement for women to become and remain fit—women like Coachman (born in 1923), the first black woman to win an Olympic gold medal.

The "herstory" of women athletes was slow to gain widespread recognition, but today there are myriad books, websites, magazines, television sportscasts, and radio broadcasts devoted to women in amateur, professional, and Olympic sports. Black women have made a profound contribution to this "herstory." While many of today's premier sports celebrities are African-American women, we want to remember those of yesteryear, as we dust off our active wear, jogging shoes, rackets, and balls, ready for the first beckons of spring.

Okodee mmowere, the talons of the eagle, symbol of strength, bravery, and power

MARCH

S	M	T	W	T	F	S
						1
2	3	4	5	6	7	8
9	10	11	12	13	14	15
16	17	18	19	20	21	22
$^{23}/_{30}$ $^{24}/_{31}$		25	26	27	28	29

APRIL

S	M	T	W	T	F	S
		1	2	3	4	5
6	7	8	9	10	11	12
13	14	15	16	17	18	19
20	21	22	23	24	25	26
27	28	29	30			

MARCH 2003

24 Monday

8

9

10

11

12

1

2

3

4

5

6

25 Tuesday

Slave trade abolished in England 1807
Toni Cade Bambara born 1939
Aretha Franklin born 1942

8

9

10

11

12

1

2

3

4

5

6

26 Wednesday

Diana Ross born 1944

8

9

10

11

12

1

2

3

4

5

6

"Rarely are colleagues, opera and concert managers, conductors, impresarios, executives of recording and television studios, press and publicity agents, stage managers as well as stagehands so completely in accord about a single individual. Somehow, she reflects her immense talent and the great confidence she has in herself on others."

–Hugh Lee Lyon, referring to Leontyne Price, from *Leontyne Price: Highlights of a Prima Donna*

The legacy of musical women is that they reflect their gifts on us, making us all the better for it. While black music lovers are sometimes book lovers, research has shown that African-American book lovers are very often music lovers, also. For this special subset, the next best thing to listening to a musical woman is reading about her.

MARCH 24 - 30

27 Thursday

Leroy Carr born 1905
Harold Nicholas born 1921
Sarah Vaughn born 1924
Arthur Mitchell born 1934

8

9

10

11

12

1

2

3

4

5

6

28 Friday

8

9

10

11

12

1

2

3

4

5

6

29 Saturday

Pearl Bailey born 1918

30 Sunday

Proclamation made of the ratification of
the 15TH Amendment 1870

Happily, volumes and volumes are in print covering artists in every musical tradition from the operatic Price to the queens of soul and hip hop—Aretha and Latifah. And while for generations, voice has been the instrument of choice—or necessity—black women today are increasingly members, even leaders, of the band.

Women's History Month would not be complete without some applause for the women of note (musical note, that is) whose stories—told in memoir or biography—have enriched us almost as much as their music. So often their wonderful gifts are not only of music but also of character—the former audible and the latter transferable by example and inspiration.

MARCH

S	M	T	W	T	F	S
						1
2	3	4	5	6	7	8
9	10	11	12	13	14	15
16	17	18	19	20	21	22
23/30	24/31	25	26	27	28	29

APRIL

S	M	T	W	T	F	S
		1	2	3	4	5
6	7	8	9	10	11	12
13	14	15	16	17	18	19
20	21	22	23	24	25	26
27	28	29	30			

31 Monday

8	
9	
10	
11	
12	
1	
2	
3	
4	
5	
6	

1 Tuesday

APRIL FOOL'S DAY
Alberta Hunter born 1895
Samuel R. Delany born 1942

8	
9	
10	
11	
12	
1	
2	
3	
4	
5	
6	

2 Wednesday

Marvin Gaye born 1939

8	
9	9:45 A.M. Dr. Byrne
10	
11	
12	
1	
2	
3	
4	
5	
6	

Men of faith place their faith not in others, not even in themselves, but in God. It is from their faith in God that their belief in themselves and trust in others first derives. As we approach the most significant remembrance of the Christian calendar—the death and resurrection of Jesus, it is a good time to reflect on the men in our lives today who are strong examples of a living faith that sacrifices self and revives others.

Think of the men who daily inspire us in ordinary, yet extraordinary, ways to seek our ultimate good in God—husbands, fathers, brothers, sons, friends, co-workers, pastors, and members of our faith communities. In a world that applauds men for strength, wealth, and position, the valor of men who cultivate and apply spiritual power to the challenges of everyday life often goes unheralded, even unnoticed. Let's note them.

And let's not allow our words to be ashes in our mouths, but instead make them words of appreciation, like cool water that refreshes, for the quiet, quotidian acts of faith by the men in our lives.

Nsoromma, the star, a symbol of loyalty to the Supreme Being and of faith, reminding us to depend on God and not ourselves

MARCH 31 – APRIL 6

3 Thursday
John Willis Menard born 1838

4 Friday
Muddy Waters born 1915
Maya Angelou born 1928

5 Saturday
Robert Smalls born 1839
Booker T. Washington born 1856
Colin Powell born 1937

8

9

10

11

12

1

2

3

4

5

6

6 Sunday
DAYLIGHT SAVING TIME BEGINS
Billy Dee Williams born 1937

"Whenever we look to find our *summum bonum*—our ultimate good—in anything less than God we are desolated to find that it almost always turns to ashes in our mouths."

**—Desmond Tutu
from *An African Prayer Book***

APRIL						
S	M	T	W	T	F	S
		1	2	3	4	5
6	7	8	9	10	11	12
13	14	15	16	17	18	19
20	21	22	23	24	25	26
27	28	29	30			

MAY						
S	M	T	W	T	F	S
				1	2	3
4	5	6	7	8	9	10
11	12	13	14	15	16	17
18	19	20	21	22	23	24
25	26	27	28	29	30	31

APRIL 2003

7 Monday

Billie Holiday born 1915

8
9
10
11
12
1
2
3
4
5
6

8 Tuesday

Kofi Annan born 1938
First black page appointed to the Senate
    1965
Suzan-Lori Parks wins Pulitzer Prize for
    Drama for *Topdog/Underdog* 2002

8
9
10
11
12
1
2
3
4
5
6

9 Wednesday

Civil War ends 1865
Paul Robeson born 1898
Paule Marshall born 1929
First black page appointed to the
    House 1965

8
9
10
11
12
1
2
3
4
5
6

" AFRICAN METHODISTS ARGUED THAT . . .
THERE SHOULD BE A UNION OF ALL METHODISTS
BECAUSE GOD WAS COLOR-BLIND, BUT AS LONG
AS SOME MEN CHERISHED THEIR WHITENESS,
AFRICAN METHODISTS WOULD SHOW THEM
THROUGH SCHOLARSHIP THAT BLACKNESS
TOO COULD BE EXALTED."

—William Seraile
from *Fire in His Heart: Bishop Benjamin Tucker Tanner and the A.M.E. Church*

APRIL 7 - 13

10 Thursday

Noah Ryder born 1914

8 _____

9 _____

10 _____

11 _____

12 _____

1 _____

2 _____

3 _____

4 _____

5 _____

6 _____

11 Friday

Spelman College established 1881
Percy L. Julian born 1899

8 _____

9 _____

10 _____

11 _____

12 _____

1 _____

2 _____

3 _____

4 _____

5 _____

6 _____

12 Saturday

Johnny Dodds born 1892
Horace Roscoe Cayton, Jr. born 1903
Lionel Hampton born 1908

13 Sunday

PALM SUNDAY
Nella Larsen born 1891

The days leading up to Easter are good ones during which to reflect on the religious institutions that have sustained Africans in America these 400 years. Such organizations, which were almost exclusively Christian until fifty years ago and still remain overwhelmingly Christian, have not only been the spiritual anchor of black communities, but often their political, cultural, and educational compasses, as well.

Yet "institutional religion" is sometimes an unpopular concept these days, with many preferring to be spiritual in their own way.

Imagine the course of progress for Africans in America if the founders of the great black denominations and churches, founded by those determined freedmen and women and those valiant formerly enslaved individuals who had escaped or bought their freedom, had each decided to be spiritual in their own personal way, rather than to bond together and establish enduring institutions.

Their faith was deeply personal. The work that grew out of their faith was, thankfully for us, widely corporate.

APRIL						
S	M	T	W	T	F	S
		1	2	3	4	5
6	7	8	9	10	11	12
13	14	15	16	17	18	19
20	21	22	23	24	25	26
27	28	29	30			

MAY						
S	M	T	W	T	F	S
				1	2	3
4	5	6	7	8	9	10
11	12	13	14	15	16	17
18	19	20	21	22	23	24
25	26	27	28	29	30	31

APRIL 2003

14 Monday
Gene Ammons born 1925

8

9

10

11

12

1

2

3

4

5

6

15 Tuesday
A. Philip Randolph born 1889
Bessie Smith born 1894?
Elizabeth Catlett born 1915?
Evelyn Ashford born 1957

8

9

10

11

12

1

2

3

4

5

6

16 Wednesday
PASSOVER BEGINS AT SUNDOWN

8

9

10

11

12

1

2

3

4

5

6

"African Americans' spirituality is woven into the texture of everyday living. Their knowledge and use of the Bible is a significant resource that helped their ancestors make meaning out of dehumanizing conditions in the slave society. That meaning is enriched through their identification with biblical characters and the story of the drama of the divine-human encounter."

—Michael I. N. Dash
from *Holy Bible: The African American Jubilee Edition*

Religion has been defined as man's seeking for God. The Bible, however, is the revelation of God's seeking for man. Poll after poll has shown that black people in America, more than any other group in the nation, are participants in this "divine-human encounter." Easter, for us, is not a religious date on a calendar, but a celebration of the event

APRIL 14 – 20

17 Thursday

8

9

10

11

12

1

2

3

4

5

6

18 Friday

GOOD FRIDAY
Eurreal "Little Brother" Montgomery
born 1906

8

9

10

11

12

1

2

3

4

5

6

19 Saturday

Etheridge Knight born 1931

20 Sunday ✝

EASTER
Carrie Mae Weems born 1953

that made our encounter possible.

Because our individual encounter with the divine is guided by the Bible, we can be encouraged by the exciting biblical and historical research that is documenting and proving what many have long believed: that the Bible and the Christian faith it underpins were *not* first introduced to enslaved Africans in America. Rather, Christianity, with its origins in northern Africa and the Middle East, spread south to Africa a thousand years before Colonialists brought Euro-centric Christianity to the Americas.

Not only is the Bible part of the texture of "everyday living" for many of us, it is part of our roots.

		APRIL				
S	M	T	W	T	F	S
		1	2	3	4	5
6	7	8	9	10	11	12
13	14	15	16	17	18	19
20	21	22	23	24	25	26
27	28	29	30			

		MAY				
S	M	T	W	T	F	S
				1	2	3
4	5	6	7	8	9	10
11	12	13	14	15	16	17
18	19	20	21	22	23	24
25	26	27	28	29	30	31

APRIL 2003

21 Monday

22 Tuesday
EARTH DAY
Charles Mingus born 1922

23 Wednesday
Jimmie Noone born 1895
Charles Johnson born 1948

21 Monday	22 Tuesday	23 Wednesday
8	8	8
9	9	9
10	10	10
11	11	11
12	12	12
1	1	1
2	2	2
3	3	3
4	4	4
5	5	5
6	6	6

"To become a successful gospel singer, you have to have the gospel in your heart. Being a gospel singer is more than just a talent, more than just a gift. It's having that spirit."

—Cece Winans
from *Sepia Dreams: A Celebration of Black Achievement Through Words and Images*
by Matthew Jordan Smith and Dionne Bennett

The glow of Resurrection Sunday is still with many of us book lovers, whom surveys have shown are often also appreciative of gospel music. This post-Easter week, we may tune our radios to a gospel station or pop one of our favorite CDs or cassettes into the player. As we listen, or even if we just hum an oft-repeated tune, it's a good time to reflect on the meaning the music conveys.

Winans succinctly states that having the gospel in one's "heart" and "having

APRIL 21 - 27

24 Thursday

Johnny Griffin born 1928

25 Friday

NATIONAL ARBOR DAY
Ella Fitzgerald born 1918?
Albert King born 1923

26 Saturday

Ma Rainey born 1886

24 Thursday	25 Friday
8	8
9	9
10	10
11	11
12	12
1	1
2	2
3	3
4	4
5	5
6	6

27 Sunday

Jesse Redmon Fauset born 1882
Coretta Scott King born 1927
August Wilson born 1945

that spirit" are at the core of African-American Christian musical styles.

The "heart" in that traditional parlance is the seat of emotion. The message of the gospels embodied in this music is to be used to shape our emotions. Just as we can be in charge of our words and actions, we can take control of our emotions. We need not become, and certainly need not remain, fearful, angry, sad, or frustrated. Gospel artists minister to our emotions and show us how to bring our moods and feelings under control.

"Spirit" is the human essence connected with the living God proclaimed by the gospels. Having the spirit may well be evidenced by a rousing reaction to gospel music, but it is so much more than that. The spirit actually leads the music down the pathway to an encounter with the divine.

We celebrate gospel artists as cultural innovators who lead us far beyond where we can go with our ears.

APRIL

S	M	T	W	T	F	S
		1	2	3	4	5
6	7	8	9	10	11	12
13	14	15	16	17	18	19
20	21	22	23	24	25	26
27	28	29	30			

MAY

S	M	T	W	T	F	S
				1	2	3
4	5	6	7	8	9	10
11	12	13	14	15	16	17
18	19	20	21	22	23	24
25	26	27	28	29	30	31

APRIL - MAY 2003

28 Monday

29 Tuesday
Duke Ellington born 1899

30 Wednesday

28 Monday	29 Tuesday	30 Wednesday
8	8	8
9	9	9 Dr. Byrne 9:00
10	10	10
11	11	11
12	12	12
1	1	1
2	2	2
3	3	3
4	4	4
5	5	5
6	6	6

"IMAGINE AFRICAN-AMERICAN MEN AND WOMEN, EXHAUSTED FROM SUNUP-TO-SUNDOWN HARD SLAVE LABOR, SINGING THEMSELVES TO EXUBERANCE—TO LIFE! THIS SONG OF DELIVERANCE, OF VICTORY OVER EMOTIONAL AND PHYSICAL OPPRESSION, SERVED THEM WELL. AFTER A NIGHT OF 'PRAYING THROUGH' (PRAYING UNTIL THEY FELT THEY HAD TOUCHED THE HEART OF GOD AND BEEN TOUCHED IN RETURN), THEY COULD LAY DOWN THEIR BURDENS AND FACE THE NEXT DAY WITH RENEWED STRENGTH."

—Gwendolin Sims Warren
from *Ev'ry Time I Feel the Spirit*

APRIL 28 – MAY 4

1 Thursday
NATIONAL DAY OF PRAYER
Sterling Brown born 1901

8

9

10

11

12

1

2

3

4

5

6

2 Friday
Nannie Helen Burroughs born 1879

8

9

10

11

12

1

2

3

4

5

6

3 Saturday
James Brown born 1933
Kimberla Lawson Roby born 1965

4 Sunday

While we are still basking in the glory of Easter, prayer may not feel essential, yet it is often when the need to pray is not so apparent that this blessed communication has its most mystical power.

Our enslaved ancestors created a legacy of prayer that survives in African America today. While our prayers may not be for deliverance from oppression, though that need remains in pernicious ways, we must still "pray through" our circumstances—whether times are sweet or bitter, relaxed or challenging. Our prayers can be likened to the electricity that flows when a plug meets a power socket; prayer is a conduit for God's power.

Prayer is an important tradition to maintain because prayers of praise, thanksgiving, forgiveness, intercession, and request—all the various kinds of prayer—keep the power of God flowing in us.

APRIL						
S	M	T	W	T	F	S
		1	2	3	4	5
6	7	8	9	10	11	12
13	14	15	16	17	18	19
20	21	22	23	24	25	26
27	28	29	30			

MAY						
S	M	T	W	T	F	S
				1	2	3
4	5	6	7	8	9	10
11	12	13	14	15	16	17
18	19	20	21	22	23	24
25	26	27	28	29	30	31

MAY 2003

5 Monday
Adam Clayton Powell, Sr. born 1865

8

9

10

11

12

1

2

3

4

5

6

6 Tuesday
Martin R. Delany born 1812
Willie Mays born 1931

8

9

10

11

12

1

2

3

4

5

6

7 Wednesday

8

9

10

11

12

1

2

3

4

5

6

" 'Where is she?' [Paul D.]
'Dead.' [Sethe]
'Aw no. When?'
'Eight years now.
    Almost nine.'
'Was it hard? I hope she
    didn't die hard.'
Sethe shook her head.
'Soft as cream. Being
    alive was the hard
    part.' "

—from *Beloved*
by Toni Morrison

Motherhood is far from easy, and mothering African Americans certainly has special challenges and unique beauty. Black fiction depicts a wide array of mothers and, while these characters are creations of the imagination, they offer much to reflect upon as we approach Mother's Day.

Sethe, Toni Morrison's memorable mother in the novel *Beloved*, who takes her child's life rather than see

MAY 5 - 11

8 Thursday

Mary Lou Williams born 1910

8 _____
9 _____
10 _____
11 _____
12 _____
1 _____
2 _____
3 _____
4 _____
5 _____
6 _____

9 Friday

Rudolph Fisher born 1897

8 _____
9 _____
10 _____
11 _____
12 _____
1 _____
2 _____
3 _____
4 _____
5 _____
6 _____

10 Saturday

P.B.S. Pinchback born 1837
Judith Jamison born 1943

_____
_____
_____
_____
_____
_____

11 Sunday

MOTHER'S DAY
King Oliver born 1885
William Grant Still born 1895

_____
_____
_____
_____

her grow up to be a slave, is either the epitome or nadir of mother love, depending on one's perspective. As with the best of mothers, Sethe equally embodies the horrors of slavery and the relentless caring of black motherhood. She is instructive to us when we appreciate African-American mothers today, for our mothering so often reflects our circumstances, making our expressions of love splendidly intricate and all the more valuable.

MAY						
S	M	T	W	T	F	S
				1	2	3
4	5	6	7	8	9	10
11	12	13	14	15	16	17
18	19	20	21	22	23	24
25	26	27	28	29	30	31

JUNE						
S	M	T	W	T	F	S
1	2	3	4	5	6	7
8	9	10	11	12	13	14
15	16	17	18	19	20	21
22	23	24	25	26	27	28
29	30					

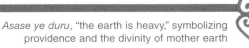

Asase ye duru, "the earth is heavy," symbolizing providence and the divinity of mother earth

MAY 2003

12 Monday
Albert L. Murray born 1916
Ving Rhames born 1961

8

9

10

11

12

1

2

3

4

5

6

13 Tuesday
Stevie Wonder born 1950

8

9

10

11

12

1

2

3

4

5

6

14 Wednesday
Sidney Bechet born 1897

8

9

10

11

12

1

2

3

4

5

6

"In *Mother Love* . . . Dove takes her explorations of relationships into the realm of Greek myth. In a series of sonnets, she examines the mother-daughter love between Demeter and Persephone."

—from *The Norton Anthology of African American Literature*
Henry Louis Gates, Jr. and Nellie Y. McKay, General Editors

Mother Love, Rita Dove's 1995 book of poems, is an innovative marriage of Greek mythology and African-American tradition. As book lovers, we are always enriched when writers expand our horizons and help us see our journey as one wonderful expression of the human condition.

MAY 12 - 18

15 Thursday
Alvin Poussaint born 1934

8

9

10

11

12

1

2

3

4

5

6

16 Friday
Betty Carter born 1930

8

9

10

11

12

1

2

3

4

5

6

17 Saturday
ARMED FORCES DAY

18 Sunday
Joseph Turner born 1911

Mother-daughter relationships are special because so often they are a triad. Every woman who has a daughter is a triune being, at once mother and daughter and self. As we give and receive honor as mothers, we have a unique opportunity to live what poets can only sadly approximate in even the best verse: the joy of repetition and erasure. Every mother's joy is passing on the wonderful things her mother taught her and obliterating from her unconscious the words, attitudes, and actions she wishes to lock out of her daughter's experience.

African-American mother-daughter relationships are among the sweetest and most complex and dynamic we can ever experience and our poets and writers constantly help us explore and celebrate them.

MAY						
S	M	T	W	T	F	S
				1	2	3
4	5	6	7	8	9	10
11	12	13	14	15	16	17
18	19	20	21	22	23	24
25	26	27	28	29	30	31

JUNE						
S	M	T	W	T	F	S
1	2	3	4	5	6	7
8	9	10	11	12	13	14
15	16	17	18	19	20	21
22	23	24	25	26	27	28
29	30					

MAY 2003

19 Monday
Malcolm X born 1925
Lorraine Hansberry born 1930

8

9

10

11

12

1

2

3

4

5

6

20 Tuesday
Lydia Cabrera born 1900

8

9

10

11

12

1

2

3

4

5

6

21 Wednesday
Regina M. Anderson born 1901
Thomas Wright "Fats" Waller born 1904

8

9

9:45 appt Dr. Byrn

10

11

12

1

2

3

4

5

6

"I have often reflected upon the new vistas that reading opened to me. I knew right there in prison that reading had changed forever the course of my life. As I see it today, the ability to read awoke inside me some long dormant craving to be mentally alive."

—Malcolm X
from his autobiography

One of the many lessons El-Hajj Malik El-Shabazz taught us is that reading keeps us mentally alive. He had not celebrated his 40th birthday when his life was taken on February 21, 1965, yet, if we can take a fantastical view and measure life in book years, our beloved, well-read Malcolm was certainly an octogenarian when he died.

There are many fitting ways to celebrate Malcolm's enduring contribution to black

MAY 19 - 25

22 Thursday

Sun Ra born 1914
Paul Winfield born 1941

8

9

10

11

12

1

2

3

4

5

6

23 Friday

William H. Carney awarded
Congressional Medal of
Honor 1900

8

9

10

11

12

1

2

3

4

5

6

24 Saturday

25 Sunday

Dorothy Porter Wesley born 1905
Miles Davis born 1926
Jamaica Kincaid born 1949

---

liberation, and one way is to resurrect him mentally—let him speak to us by reading his books and speeches. Books are to thoughts as bodies are to spirits, anchors to this world. As long as we can read Malcolm, his thoughts live, and he enlivens us mentally.

While the content of much that is being published and read in the current black book renaissance would probably displease Malcolm, the existence of such a vibrant reading component in today's African-American lifestyles would likely gladden him. Books have freed some imprisoned part of the mind of every voracious reader, unshackling visions, expanding horizons. His exhortation to read remains one of the myriad gifts Malcolm gave to the struggle for liberation.

MAY						
S	M	T	W	T	F	S
				1	2	3
4	5	6	7	8	9	10
11	12	13	14	15	16	17
18	19	20	21	22	23	24
25	26	27	28	29	30	31

JUNE						
S	M	T	W	T	F	S
1	2	3	4	5	6	7
8	9	10	11	12	13	14
15	16	17	18	19	20	21
22	23	24	25	26	27	28
29	30					

MAY – JUNE 2003

26 Monday
MEMORIAL DAY OBSERVED

8

9

10

11

12

1

2

3

4

5

6

27 Tuesday
Louis Gossett, Jr. born 1936

8

9

10

11

12

1

2

3

4

5

6

28 Wednesday
Aaron "T-Bone" Walker born 1910

8

9

10

11

12

1

2

3

4

5

6

"Some time I feel that you and I were never as close, heart and heart as we should be, but I have loved you very dearly and if I failed in some things it was lack of knowledge."

—Carrie Langston Hughes
from *The Life of Langston Hughes* by Arnold Rampersad

For Americans of African descent, the relationship between mothers and children is historically bittersweet. Sweet, as we honor our mothers with gratitude for their essential role in our survival these 400 years on this continent. Bitter, as mothers sometimes hold themselves responsible for circumstances far beyond their control.

In his eloquent poem "Mother to Son," Langston Hughes's deep empathy with his mother is expressed in his comparison of her life to a staircase that is splintered, boarded, uncarpeted, and certainly not crystal. This now-classic poem, written when Hughes was just 20

MAY 26 - JUNE 1

29 Thursday

8 _____
9 _____
10 _____
11 _____
12 _____
1 _____
2 _____
3 _____
4 _____
5 _____
6 _____

30 Friday

Countee Cullen born 1903
James Earl Chaney born 1943

8 _____
9 _____
10 _____
11 _____
12 _____
1 _____
2 _____
3 _____
4 _____
5 _____
6 _____

31 Saturday

Shirley Verrett born 1931

1 Sunday

Morgan Freeman born 1937

---

years old, reflects the sweetness with which black mothers are regarded, the compassion with which their children understand their struggles.

Compare Hughes's poem to his mother's words. She expresses the view our beloved maternal giants often hold about themselves. We glimpse a dichotomy of our culture, between how offspring view their mothers and those mothers sometimes see themselves.

For those ripped from the bosom of the motherland, those sold away from their enslaved mothers, those challenged under the weight of oppression, past and present, an invincible mother love has been a major sustaining element of our heritage.

May the writings of Hughes and so many other African-American authors who have explored the topic of motherhood, help mothers discover they are loved and accepted, not for an unattainable perfection, but because they have, by example, inspired victory.

MAY						
S	M	T	W	T	F	S
				1	2	3
4	5	6	7	8	9	10
11	12	13	14	15	16	17
18	19	20	21	22	23	24
25	26	27	28	29	30	31

JUNE						
S	M	T	W	T	F	S
1	2	3	4	5	6	7
8	9	10	11	12	13	14
15	16	17	18	19	20	21
22	23	24	25	26	27	28
29	30					

JUNE 2003

2 Monday

John Hope born 1868
Dorothy West born 1907
Cornel West born 1953

8

9

10

11

12

1

2

3

4

5

6

3 Tuesday

Roland Hayes born 1887
Charles Richard Drew born 1904
Josephine Baker born 1906

8

9

10

11

12

1

2

3

4

5

6

4 Wednesday

8

9

10

11

12

1

2

3

4

5

6

He'd been raised to be useful. Manhood Training, his father called it when he taught him how to mow the lawn, take out the trash, repair the car or change a tire, and make sure his two younger sisters were 'guarded' at all times. 'Ladies look to men to take care of them. There's a lot of benefits if you do it right.' When Satchel would grumble about his early-morning paper route ('So you'll learn responsibility'), or having to shovel the snow ('So your mother and sisters won't slip and fall'), his father would say, 'Son, one day when you have a family of your own, you'll thank me for this.' "

—from *Singing in the Comeback Choir*
by Bebe Moore Campbell

JUNE 2 - 8

5 Thursday

Marion Motley born 1920

8

9

10

11

12

1

2

3

4

5

6

6 Friday

A'Lelia Walker born 1885
Marian Wright Edelman born 1939

8

9

10

11

12

1

2

3

4

5

6

7 Saturday

Gwendolyn Brooks born 1917
Nikki Giovanni born 1943

8 Sunday

PENTECOST

When it comes to finding good African-American fathers, most of us don't have to look to fiction, and although few novelists write about this aspect of black life better than Campbell, it's evident that she sketches her rich father characters from her own father. Her memoir, *Sweet Summer: Growing Up With and Without My Dad*, portrays her father as a wonderfully consistent, present, and shaping influence in her life despite his divorce from her mother, residence in another state, and obvious personal failings.

Campbell is able to draw on the richness of his fathering to create her father characters because she understands that being a great dad means living out the three positive qualities mentioned above, *not* being perfect, or even having the ideal relationship with Mom.

While we have wonderful father figures in African-American fiction, let's not hold our real-life dads up to fiction standards. Let's celebrate them for who they are.

JUNE						
S	M	T	W	T	F	S
1	2	3	4	5	6	7
8	9	10	11	12	13	14
15	16	17	18	19	20	21
22	23	24	25	26	27	28
29	30					

JULY						
S	M	T	W	T	F	S
		1	2	3	4	5
6	7	8	9	10	11	12
13	14	15	16	17	18	19
20	21	22	23	24	25	26
27	28	29	30	31		

Akoko nan, the hen's feet, symbol of protectiveness and parental discipline tempered with patience, mercy, and fondness

JUNE 2003

9 Monday
T. D. Jakes born 1957

10 Tuesday
Hattie McDaniel born 1895

11 Wednesday
Hazel Scott born 1920

9 Monday	10 Tuesday	11 Wednesday
8	8	8
9	9	9
10	10	10
11	11	11
12	12	12
1	1	1
2	2	2
3	3	3
4	4	4
5	5	5
6	6	6

"As a community, we need to hold up examples of fathers and other male figures who are functioning well and trying to give their sons positive fathering. We applaud those African American males who grew up with excellent role models and father figures, and are now giving something back to our communities by becoming mentors and role models for boys who have not been as fortunate."

—Nancy Boyd-Franklin, Ph.D. and A. J. Franklin, Ph.D.
from *Boys into Men: Raising Our African American Teenage Sons*

JUNE 9 - 15

12 Thursday

8 _____

9 _____

10 _____

11 _____

12 _____

1 _____

2 _____

3 _____

4 _____

5 _____

6 _____

13 Friday

Eleanor Holmes Norton born 1937

8 _____

9 _____

10 _____

11 _____

12 _____

1 _____

2 _____

3 _____

4 _____

5 _____

6 _____

14 Saturday

FLAG DAY
Harriet Beecher Stowe born 1811
John Edgar Wideman born 1941

15 Sunday

FATHER'S DAY

Many African Americans who grow up in single-mom households actually have an abundance of fathers, even in the absence of a blood father. This is because so many of our great dads are not only parenting their own children, but their grandchildren, nieces, nephews, and other relatives, or other kids who are no blood relation but are in their churches, neighborhoods, or volunteer organizations. These mentor-fathers deserve special celebration.

But nothing—no giant greeting card, not even the biggest hug, or his favorite home-cooked dinner—can repay the debt these everyday heroes have accumulated in the life ledgers of those they've parented. The only way we can repay them is to imitate them by mentor-parenting the youth in need whose paths we cross.

This Father's Day, let's not only show mentor-fathers the best love and gratitude we know how, but also ask them for pointers, so they can inspire us to make their fire an ongoing flame of our heritage.

JUNE						
S	M	T	W	T	F	S
1	2	3	4	5	6	7
8	9	10	11	12	13	14
15	16	17	18	19	20	21
22	23	24	25	26	27	28
29	30					

JULY						
S	M	T	W	T	F	S
		1	2	3	4	5
6	7	8	9	10	11	12
13	14	15	16	17	18	19
20	21	22	23	24	25	26
27	28	29	30	31		

JUNE 2003

16 Monday

Lucky Thompson born 1924

8 _____
9 _____
10 _____
11 _____
12 _____
1 _____
2 _____
3 _____
4 _____
5 _____
6 _____

17 Tuesday

James Weldon Johnson born 1871
Venus Williams born 1980

8 _____
9 _____
10 _____
11 _____
12 _____
1 _____
2 _____
3 _____
4 _____
5 _____
6 _____

18 Wednesday

8 _____
9 _____
10 *Dr. appt Dr Bepal*
11 _____
12 _____
1 _____
2 _____
3 _____
4 _____
5 _____
6 _____

"[H]e approaches with a brisk, toes-out stride. He is whistling and stops to greet the druggist, the baker, our building super, almost everybody he passes. To some kids on the block, he is a faintly comical figure. Not to me. This jaunty, confident little man is Luther Powell, my father."

—Colin Powell
from *My American Journey*

It's been said that behind every great man there's a woman, but just as true is that *preceding* every great man is a father. "Dad" is one of the most under-sung figures in the heritage of African Americans. In fact, black fathers have been given a bad image in the media, and even in responding to some of the best novels penned by black writers, reviewers and readers have forgotten that the brutal, deserting father is *fiction*.

JUNE 16 - 22

19 Thursday
JUNETEENTH

20 Friday
Charles Waddell Chesnutt born 1858
Eric Dolphy born 1928

21 Saturday
SUMMER SOLSTICE
Joseph Hayne Rainey born 1832
Henry Ossawa Tanner born 1859

8 _____

9 _____

10 _____

11 _____

12 _____

1 _____

2 _____

3 _____

4 _____

5 _____

6 _____

8 _____

9 _____

10 _____

11 _____

12 _____

1 _____

2 _____

3 _____

4 _____

5 _____

6 _____

22 Sunday
Katherine Dunham born 1910
Ed Bradley born 1941
Octavia Butler born 1947

A survey of nonfiction, especially memoir, by African Americans reveals a pattern that is reality, and black fathers are among the most beloved figures of the culture.

Powell's words about his dad are touching because they reveal his respect for the quirky individuality of his father. That uniqueness of personality is found over and over in fathers portrayed in the memoirs of our most prominent figures. Black fathers defy stereotype. They are not cookie-cutter dads. They certainly are not "Father Knows Best" imitations in black. If there is any racial signature black men have placed on fatherhood in this country, it's the maintenance of self, the preservation of unique wholeness, leadership of the family, but not losing oneself in it. What a gift. The example of being one's own person is an inspiration to know and be oneself, and that is a prerequisite to survival against the odds and a main ingredient of greatness.

JUNE						
S	M	T	W	T	F	S
1	2	3	4	5	6	7
8	9	10	11	12	13	14
15	16	17	18	19	20	21
22	23	24	25	26	27	28
29	30					

JULY						
S	M	T	W	T	F	S
		1	2	3	4	5
6	7	8	9	10	11	12
13	14	15	16	17	18	19
20	21	22	23	24	25	26
27	28	29	30	31		

JUNE 2003

23 Monday

Milt Hinton born 1910
Wilma Rudolph born 1940

8

9

10

11

12

1

2

3

4

5

6

24 Tuesday

8

9

10

11

12

1

2

3

4

5

6

25 Wednesday

8

9

10

11

12

1

2

3

4

5

6

"So I went home with the cast and I stayed out of school eight weeks. Granddad came to see me again, kissed me on the forehead, and rubbed my arm. And he gave me a quarter. . . . and said: 'Get yourself some ice cream. It's got calcium in it.'"

—Bill Cosby
from *Cosbyology*

Cosby's grandfather had warned him not to play football. When he broke his arm at the game, the quote above was his granddad's good-natured reaction.

No month of reflections on fatherhood would be complete without Black Ameri-

JUNE 23 - 29

26 Thursday

William Lee "Big Bill" Broonzy
born 1893

8

9

10

11

12

1

2

3

4

5

6

27 Friday

Paul Laurence Dunbar born 1872
M. Carl Holman born 1919
Lucille Clifton born 1936

8

9

10

11

12

1

2

3

4

5

6

28 Saturday

29 Sunday

James Van Der Zee born 1886
Stokely Carmichael born 1941

ca's poster dad Cosby and a salute to grandfathers. All can be counted on for a laugh, and once the chuckle is past, a bit of wisdom always remains.

The sagacity of grandfathers shows when they know we won't listen to their advice and they give it anyway. The glory of grandfathers is revealed when they give us a kiss and a quarter after our failure to listen gets us into trouble. The love of grandfathers is expressed when they let us catch our own consequences, and refuse to smooth the bumps and scrapes we get when we choose our own rocky paths.

Each new generation of African Americans charts its own way and each generation of granddads smiles at the fresh breaks of the young with accumulated wisdom in their strong old bones.

JUNE						
S	M	T	W	T	F	S
1	2	3	4	5	6	7
8	9	10	11	12	13	14
15	16	17	18	19	20	21
22	23	24	25	26	27	28
29	30					

JULY						
S	M	T	W	T	F	S
		1	2	3	4	5
6	7	8	9	10	11	12
13	14	15	16	17	18	19
20	21	22	23	24	25	26
27	28	29	30	31		

JUNE - JULY 2003

30 Monday

Lena Horne born 1917
Florence Ballard born 1943

8

9

10

11

12

1

2

3

4

5

6

1 Tuesday

Benjamin O. Davis, Sr. born 1877
Thomas A. Dorsey born 1899
Willie Dixon born 1915

8

9

10

11

12

1

2

3

4

5

6

2 Wednesday

Richard Nugent born 1906
Thurgood Marshall born 1908
Medgar Evers born 1925
Ed Bullins born 1935

8

9

10

11

12

1

2

3

4

5

6

I have not written my experiences in order to attract attention to myself; on the contrary, it would have been more pleasant to me to have been silent about my own history. Neither do I care to excite sympathy for my own sufferings. But I do earnestly desire to arouse the women of the North to a realizing sense of the condition of two millions of women at the South, still in bondage, suffering what I suffered, and most of them far worse. I want to add my testimony to that of abler pens to convince the people of the Free States what Slavery really is."

—Harriet Jacobs
from *Incidents in the Life of a Slave Girl*

Nkyimkyim, the zigzags, symbolizing toughness, adaptability, devotion to service, and ability to withstand hardships

JUNE 30 – JULY 6

3 Thursday

8 _____
9 _____
10 _____
11 _____
12 _____
1 _____
2 _____
3 _____
4 _____
5 _____
6 _____

4 Friday

INDEPENDENCE DAY
Tuskegee Normal School opens 1881

8 _____
9 _____
10 _____
11 _____
12 _____
1 _____
2 _____
3 _____
4 _____
5 _____
6 _____

5 Saturday

_____
_____
_____
_____

6 Sunday

Randall Robinson born 1941
Virginia DeBerry born 1949

_____
_____
_____
_____

African-American book lovers have a wide range of reading tastes, but most of us do not read much about slavery. In another decade we will celebrate the sesquicentennial of Emancipation, yet, in some ways it is still uncomfortable for us, descendants of the enslaved, to visit that period in our history.

But it is important not to forget any portion of history, even the painful ones, and by reading our earliest published writers we can discover our long heritage of resistance to oppression and struggle for freedom. Those true stories—sometimes of success even in the worst of conditions—offer many lessons. They can fuel our efforts for power and equality today and show us that there has always been a remnant of white Americans who joined with us in struggle.

Jacobs's story is particularly encouraging. She escaped from slavery in the early 1840s and worked for a white New York family who later "purchased" her freedom from Southern slave holders.

Reading the few still-existing centuries-old narratives by formerly enslaved writers is the best way to truly connect with the victors of our history. They can bring pride and fuel our energies for today's challenges.

JULY						
S	M	T	W	T	F	S
		1	2	3	4	5
6	7	8	9	10	11	12
13	14	15	16	17	18	19
20	21	22	23	24	25	26
27	28	29	30	31		

AUGUST						
S	M	T	W	T	F	S
					1	2
3	4	5	6	7	8	9
10	11	12	13	14	15	16
17	18	19	20	21	22	23
24/31	25	26	27	28	29	30

JULY 2003

7 Monday
Margaret Walker born 1915
Eric Jerome Dickey born 1961

8

9

10

11

12

1

2

3

4

5

6

8 Tuesday
Billy Eckstine born 1914

8

9

10

11

12

1

2

3

4

5

6

9 Wednesday
June Jordan born 1936

8

9

10

11

12

1

2

3

4

5

6

"Nighttime became a horrible nightmare. The cries of the people rose, with utterances of sorrow that filled the air. An enslaved woman interpreted her people's lamentations and anguish, describing the noise and the howling as 'owing to their having dreamt they were in their own country and finding themselves, when awake, in the hold of a slave ship.' "

—Velma Maia Thomas
from *Lest We Forget: The Passage from Africa to Slavery and Emancipation*

Summer is the time for vacation travel for most African Americans and a large percentage of us will take a bus, train, ship, or plane or just pile with family or friends into a car and drive to a family reunion, religious convocation, social convention, or a special place for leisure activity, rest, or fun.

JULY 7 - 13

10 Thursday

Arthur Ashe born 1943

8

9

10

11

12

1

2

3

4

5

6

11 Friday

8

9

10

11

12

1

2

3

4

5

6

12 Saturday

Bill Cosby born 1937

13 Sunday

Wole Soyinka born 1934
Albert Ayler born 1936

JULY						
S	M	T	W	T	F	S
		1	2	3	4	5
6	7	8	9	10	11	12
13	14	15	16	17	18	19
20	21	22	23	24	25	26
27	28	29	30	31		

AUGUST						
S	M	T	W	T	F	S
					1	2
3	4	5	6	7	8	9
10	11	12	13	14	15	16
17	18	19	20	21	22	23
24/31	25	26	27	28	29	30

We all hope to depart and return with "traveling mercies" and as we lift those pre-travel prayer requests, we can be mindful that we are already the beneficiaries of the greatest traveling mercies ever to flow upon human beings. We descended from survivors of the cruelest, most inhuman journey devised by the wicked edges of the human heart. Traveling mercies are a blessing passed down to us.

While the memory of terror has dampened travel for many these past few years, it's encouraging to acknowledge that we have a much older, more horrible memory that can actually provide us with a positive view of travel: that we leave, arrive, and return by the mercies of God.

JULY 2003

14 Monday

15 Tuesday
Philly Joe Jones born 1923

16 Wednesday
Ida Bell Wells-Barnett born 1862
Mari Evans born 1923

14 Monday	15 Tuesday	16 Wednesday
8	8	8
9	9	9
10	10	10
11	11	11
12	12	12
1	1	1
2	2	2
3	3	3
4	4	4
5	5	5
6	6	6

"Every folk song, verse, and melody is the product of the folk community. The community supplies its themes and its subject matter. Its unique language has been previously grown in the community's own soil and under the community's atmosphere and weather conditions. Within the community, and nowhere else, are its conventions, its social, moral, theological, and legal principles, its open and hidden prides and prejudices."

—John Lovell, Jr.
from *Black Song: The Forge and the Flame:
The Story of How the Afro-American Spiritual Was Hammered Out*

JULY 14 - 20

17 Thursday
Diahann Carroll born 1935

8

9

10

11

12

1

2

3

4

5

6

18 Friday
Nelson Mandela born 1918

8

9

10

11

12

1

2

3

4

5

6

19 Saturday
Alice Dunbar Nelson born 1875

20 Sunday
Henry Dumas born 1934

There is still nothing like hearing an old "Negro Spiritual." During these dog days of summer heat, nothing cools like one of those old songs born in the heat of oppression, under the hot sun of forced labor.

Whether we're sick and tired, or just sick and tired of whatever our situation is, these bars of music and their simple words bring solace. They minister to grief and explode pent-up feelings, allowing free expression. They create transcendent silence when hummed from deep in the belly. This is our heritage, part of a vibrant culture born despite slavery.

The scars of that horror are in our psychological DNA, etched into our souls and psyches. But so is the healing gene that can transform the grief of our forebears into a gift for us and our progeny.

JULY						
S	M	T	W	T	F	S
		1	2	3	4	5
6	7	8	9	10	11	12
13	14	15	16	17	18	19
20	21	22	23	24	25	26
27	28	29	30	31		

AUGUST						
S	M	T	W	T	F	S
					1	2
3	4	5	6	7	8	9
10	11	12	13	14	15	16
17	18	19	20	21	22	23
24/31	25	26	27	28	29	30

JULY 2003

21 Monday

22 Tuesday
Danny Glover born 1947

23 Wednesday

8	8	8
9	9	9
10	10	10
11	11	11
12	12	12
1	1	1
2	2	2
3	3	3
4	4	4
5	5	5
6	6	6

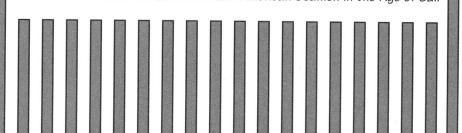

"The authorities promptly jailed him under the law requiring incarceration of free black sailors. . . . Jail expenses became considerable for ship owners who were held legally liable, and devastating for the wage-earning sailors to whom the owners passed on the cost."

—W. Jeffrey Bolster
from *Black Jacks: African American Seamen in the Age of Sail*

JULY 21 - 27

24 Thursday

Ira Aldridge born 1807
Charles Spurgeon Johnson born 1893
Kenneth Bancroft Clark born 1914

8

9

10

11

12

1

2

3

4

5

6

25 Friday

Johnny Hodges born 1906

8

9

10

11

12

1

2

3

4

5

6

26 Saturday

27 Sunday

NOTHING could be more horrid than slavery, but free blacks often had it almost as bad. A black sailor who docked at Charleston aboard the schooner *Fox* on April 22, 1823, was jailed for no other reason than being of African descent. Compare blacks sailing 180 years ago to blacks driving today.

While *de facto* practices promote the current, well-documented injustices on the roads and highways, actual laws were passed in North Carolina in the 1800s to require the incarceration of free black sailors. It was rebellion fomented by black sailors—rather than the horrors of slavery—that lawmakers believed caused the armed revolt of Nat Turner.

African Americans who were citizens before Abolition set us on the road to full human freedom, a road we continue to travel with courage and confidence.

JULY						
S	M	T	W	T	F	S
		1	2	3	4	5
6	7	8	9	10	11	12
13	14	15	16	17	18	19
20	21	22	23	24	25	26
27	28	29	30	31		

AUGUST						
S	M	T	W	T	F	S
					1	2
3	4	5	6	7	8	9
10	11	12	13	14	15	16
17	18	19	20	21	22	23
24/31	25	26	27	28	29	30

JULY – AUGUST 2003

28 Monday
Proclamation made of the ratification of the 14TH Amendment 1868

29 Tuesday
Chester Himes born 1909

30 Wednesday
Elizabeth Ross Haynes born 1883
Betye Saar born 1926
Laurence Fishburne born 1961

28 Monday	29 Tuesday	30 Wednesday
8	8	8
9	9	9
10	10	10
11	11	11
12	12	12
1	1	1
2	2	2
3	3	3
4	4	4
5	5	5
6	6	6

For many African Americans, progress feels slow. For others, the remaining racial challenges seem minor. Both ends of the spectrum deserve respect. Those who keep race as a prominent issue; those who play it down to focus on individual inclusion; and those who hold all points of view in between, all contribute to our progress.

It's important to know our history, so that we can accurately measure progress and learn important lessons when ground is lost. As elections approach and the media becomes charged with politics, let's be mindful that it is not new that blacks are participating in the political process. What is new is our sustained participation. It is with continual political activity that leaders emerge.

Staying the course often feels slow, but it eventually produces results that somehow, later, seem rapid.

JULY 28 – AUGUST 3

31 Thursday
Whitney M. Young, Jr. born 1921

1 Friday
Charles Clinton Spaulding born 1874

2 Saturday
James Baldwin born 1924

8	8	
9	9	
10	10	
11	11	
12	12	
1	1	

3 Sunday

2	2
3	3
4	4
5	5
6	6

"Between 1869 and 1901, more than 600 black men were elected to state legislatures in the South."

—Velma Maia Thomas
from *Freedom's Children:
The Passage from Emancipation
to the Great Migration*

Tabono, the oars, symbolizing strength, confidence, and persistence

JULY

S	M	T	W	T	F	S
		1	2	3	4	5
6	7	8	9	10	11	12
13	14	15	16	17	18	19
20	21	22	23	24	25	26
27	28	29	30	31		

AUGUST

S	M	T	W	T	F	S
					1	2
3	4	5	6	7	8	9
10	11	12	13	14	15	16
17	18	19	20	21	22	23
24/31	25	26	27	28	29	30

AUGUST 2003

4 Monday
Louis Armstrong born 1901

5 Tuesday

6 Wednesday
Susie King Taylor born 1848

4 Monday	5 Tuesday	6 Wednesday
8	8	8
9	9	9
10	10	10
11	11	11
12	12	12
1	1	1
2	2	2
3	3	3
4	4	4
5	5	5
6	6	6

"Through our Black Family Reunion Celebrations around the country, we have brought together millions of people—families of all compositions. Our celebrations have been lauded for creating new community energy and fostering self-help approaches to many contemporary concerns. Together we can become a more caring community, the greater extended family."

—Dorothy I. Height, National Council of Negro Women
from *The Black Family Reunion Cookbook: Recipes and Food Memories*

AUGUST 4 - 10

7 Thursday

Ralph Bunche born 1904

8 _____

9 _____

10 _____

11 _____

12 _____

1 _____

2 _____

3 _____

4 _____

5 _____

6 _____

8 Friday

Matthew Henson born 1866
Benny Carter born 1907

8 _____

9 _____

10 _____

11 _____

12 _____

1 _____

2 _____

3 _____

4 _____

5 _____

6 _____

9 Saturday

Janie Porter Barrett born 1865
Whitney Houston born 1963

10 Sunday

Anna Julia Hayward Cooper born 1858

Family reunions can be likened to a beautifully cast cornerstone of a building. Families are the building blocks of community, and family reunions are the most beautiful celebration of family.

As we prepare for upcoming gatherings, or savor memories of recent ones, we book lovers can add a special, enduring touch to them by incorporating a reading group component.

With the letters, phone calls, and e-mails that circulate to plan the reunion, suggest a book that everyone will enjoy reading, and specify a time during the reunion to discuss it as a group. A book discussion will bring family members of all ages and interests into a circle of sharing. And by talking about a book in a supportive environment, everyone can feel their opinions are valid, and that their expressions have been affirmed. (If this year's reunion is already past, suggest a book for next year's, or start family book clubs where relatives live near each other.)

Make your family one that reads together. Book bonds can strengthen blood bonds.

AUGUST

S	M	T	W	T	F	S
					1	2
3	4	5	6	7	8	9
10	11	12	13	14	15	16
17	18	19	20	21	22	23
24/31	25	26	27	28	29	30

SEPTEMBER

S	M	T	W	T	F	S
	1	2	3	4	5	6
7	8	9	10	11	12	13
14	15	16	17	18	19	20
21	22	23	24	25	26	27
28	29	30				

AUGUST 2003

11 Monday
Alex Haley born 1921

12 Tuesday

13 Wednesday
Kathleen Battle born 1948

11 Monday	12 Tuesday	13 Wednesday
8	8	8
9	9	9
10	10	10
11	11	11
12	12	12
1	1	1
2	2	2
3	3	3
4	4	4
5	5	5
6	6	6

"I have a wonderful collection of memories of our friendship. My recent attendance at the 35th Talladega College reunion aroused feelings of my appreciation of our friendship. . . . we managed to nurture our friendship through the years by writing, calling, visiting, and praying for each other."

—Otis Holloway Owens
from *Wearing Purple*

AUGUST 11 - 17

14 Thursday

Halle Berry born 1968

8

9

10

11

12

1

2

3

4

5

6

15 Friday

Samuel Coleridge-Taylor born 1875
Oscar Peterson born 1925

8

9

10

11

12

1

2

3

4

5

6

16 Saturday

Wallace Thurman born 1902
Wyatt Tee Walker born 1929
Carol Moseley-Braun born 1947
Angela Bassett born 1958

17 Sunday

Marcus Garvey born 1887

The friends made in college are for many graduates of historically black colleges and universities (HBCUs), almost as close as blood family. College reunions among HBCU graduates are becoming almost as popular as family reunions. These multi-class reunions are often a wonderful conglomeration of the old and young, with several generations of a family returning for the festivities.

For those who attended an HBCU—one need not have graduated to become an active alumnus—and have lost touch with classmates and professors, this summer is a good one to go back and search out the people who inhabit those fond college recollections and even plan a trip to the memory site.

While HBCUs are regularly applauded for their educational contributions to African America (although not regularly *enough!*), these institutions deserve a special salute for the close collegiality they have created among their graduates, a sense that endures for a lifetime and has spilled over to enrich our entire community, and the world.

AUGUST						
S	M	T	W	T	F	S
					1	2
3	4	5	6	7	8	9
10	11	12	13	14	15	16
17	18	19	20	21	22	23
24/31	25	26	27	28	29	30

SEPTEMBER						
S	M	T	W	T	F	S
	1	2	3	4	5	6
7	8	9	10	11	12	13
14	15	16	17	18	19	20
21	22	23	24	25	26	27
28	29	30				

18 Monday

Rafer Johnson born 1935

19 Tuesday

20 Wednesday

Isaac Hayes born 1942

18 Monday	19 Tuesday	20 Wednesday
8	8	8
9	9	9
10	10	10
11	11	11
12	12	12
1	1	1
2	2	2
3	3	3
4	4	4
5	5	5
6	6	6

The achievements of the nine national Pan-Hellenic organizations and their individual members are astounding when you consider the total history of oppressed Africans in America. To have created African American organizations that stressed education, philanthropy, self-improvement, and excellence, and to have them successfully thrive to this date, is a testament not only to the members of the organizations, but also to the vision of their respective founders."

—Lawrence C. Ross, Jr.
from *The Divine Nine: The History of African American Fraternities and Sororities*

AUGUST 18 - 24

21 Thursday

William James "Count" Basie born 1904
Melvin Van Peebles born 1932

8
9
10
11
12
1
2
3
4
5
6

22 Friday

John Lee Hooker born 1917

8
9
10
11
12
1
2
3
4
5
6

23 Saturday

24 Sunday

Special greetings, colors, codes of conduct—these are the most recognizable but least important aspects of black sororities and fraternities. These organizations have created a family-like network among their members that in many ways is second only to churches in African America. The lifelong bonds of friendship formed and deep, loyal caring among members are legendary, and still very much part of our culture today.

What thriving black sororities and fraternities have provided for the larger community is not only many stable, concerned individual contributors, but powerful organized efforts to render all types of service. What distinguishes fraternal groups from the many other service-oriented organizations in African America is the sense of fun and style that they bring to even the most serious endeavor. The fellowship they cultivate within their groups inevitably spills over to others, and what might once have seemed an insurmountable challenge, when addressed by black sororities and fraternities becomes a chance to pull together and laugh—even through tears—to victory.

Nkonsonkonson, a chain, symbol of unity, interdependence, brotherhood, and cooperation

AUGUST						
S	M	T	W	T	F	S
					1	2
3	4	5	6	7	8	9
10	11	12	13	14	15	16
17	18	19	20	21	22	23
24/31	25	26	27	28	29	30

SEPTEMBER						
S	M	T	W	T	F	S
	1	2	3	4	5	6
7	8	9	10	11	12	13
14	15	16	17	18	19	20
21	22	23	24	25	26	27
28	29	30				

AUGUST 2003

25 Monday
Althea Gibson born 1927
Wayne Shorter born 1933

8 _____

9 _____

10 _____

11 _____

12 _____

1 _____

2 _____

3 _____

4 _____

5 _____

6 _____

26 Tuesday
Branford Marsalis born 1960

8 _____

9 _____

10 _____

11 _____

12 _____

1 _____

2 _____

3 _____

4 _____

5 _____

6 _____

27 Wednesday
Lester Young born 1909

8 _____

9 _____

10 _____

11 _____

12 _____

1 _____

2 _____

3 _____

4 _____

5 _____

6 _____

"By the time of publication of his landmark *Souls of Black Folk* in 1903, the thirty-five-year-old Du Bois was one of the most widely read, broadly traveled, and impeccably educated men in the world."

—Henry Louis Gates, Jr. and Cornel West
from *The African-American Century*

28 Thursday

Rita Dove born 1952

8 _____

9 _____

10 _____

11 _____

12 _____

1 _____

2 _____

3 _____

4 _____

5 _____

6 _____

29 Friday

Charlie "Bird" Parker born 1920
Dinah Washington born 1924
Wyomia Tyus born 1945
Michael Jackson born 1958

8 _____

9 _____

10 _____

11 _____

12 _____

1 _____

2 _____

3 _____

4 _____

5 _____

6 _____

30 Saturday

Roy Wilkins born 1901
Kenny Dorham born 1924

31 Sunday

Eldridge Cleaver born 1935

Back-to-school thoughts beckon and we psychologically prepare ourselves and families for the return to classrooms. W.E.B. Du Bois was one of the greatest proponents of education, but even he had what many of us feel as we anticipate a new academic year—joy mixed with trepidation about school. Du Bois applied to complete his doctoral thesis in Berlin and was rejected, perhaps because of racism. Yet he went on to become a major writer and scholar of the century.

Every school year has triumphs and disappointments. Our goal is to take the lessons of both with us into successful lives. Mark Twain advised not to let school get in the way of your education. Let us, like Du Bois, see education as a holistic process that includes not only meeting the highest academic standards, but learning from every sort of experience.

AUGUST

S	M	T	W	T	F	S
					1	2
3	4	5	6	7	8	9
10	11	12	13	14	15	16
17	18	19	20	21	22	23
24/31	25	26	27	28	29	30

SEPTEMBER

S	M	T	W	T	F	S
	1	2	3	4	5	6
7	8	9	10	11	12	13
14	15	16	17	18	19	20
21	22	23	24	25	26	27
28	29	30				

SEPTEMBER 2003

1 Monday

LABOR DAY
Hiram R. Revels born 1822
Rosa Guy born 1928?
Nelson George born 1957

8

9

10

11

12

1

2

3

4

5

6

2 Tuesday

Horace Silver born 1928

8

9

10

11

12

1

2

3

4

5

6

3 Wednesday

Charles Hamilton Houston born 1895
Dorothy Leigh Maynor born 1910

8

9

10

11

12

1

2

3

4

5

6

"[T]he lessons that I learned in the home of Mrs. Ruffner were as valuable to me as any education I have ever gotten anywhere since. Even to this day I never see bits of paper scattered around a house or in the street that I do not want to pick them up at once . . . a filthy yard that I do not want to clean . . . an unpainted . . . house that I do not want to paint . . . or a button off one's clothes, or a grease-spot on them or on a floor, that I do not want to call attention to."

—Booker T. Washington
from his autobiography, *Up From Slavery*

SEPTEMBER 1 - 7

4 Thursday
Richard Wright born 1908

8

9

10

11

12

1

2

3

4

5

6

5 Friday
Frank Yerby born 1916

8

9

10

11

12

1

2

3

4

5

6

6 Saturday

7 Sunday
Jacob Lawrence born 1917
David Bradley born 1950

Education is not just listening to lofty ideas, it is inner transformation. Today Booker T. would likely be less criticized for his famous bootstrapping philosophy than for what would be labeled obsessive-compulsive neatness or perfectionism.

As scores of millions of African Americans—children, teens, undergrads, graduate students, and, yes, teachers and academics at all levels—return to school, his lesson instructs us.

We live in an age of relativism, where everything is small stuff and nobody is supposed to sweat it. Washington's words remind us that there *are* absolutes. The little things *are* worth the effort. The tidy book bag, neat locker, and organized student planner are precursors to punctuality and preparedness, which are prerequisites to success.

Far from nit-picking, caring about the little things is *win*-picking: giving heed to the details that allow this inner process called education to make its way from the outside in.

SEPTEMBER						
S	M	T	W	T	F	S
	1	2	3	4	5	6
7	8	9	10	11	12	13
14	15	16	17	18	19	20
21	22	23	24	25	26	27
28	29	30				

OCTOBER						
S	M	T	W	T	F	S
			1	2	3	4
5	6	7	8	9	10	11
12	13	14	15	16	17	18
19	20	21	22	23	24	25
26	27	28	29	30	31	

SEPTEMBER 2003

8 Monday

Buck Leonard born 1907

8

9

10

11

12

1

2

3

4

5

6

9 Tuesday

Sonia Sanchez born 1934
Otis Redding born 1941

8

9

10

11

12

1

2

3

4

5

6

10 Wednesday

John R. Lynch born 1847

8

9

10

11

12

1

2

3

4

5

6

"[S]ometimes I want to go to other places . . . like the north where people live in houses different from ours, and wear different clothes, and speak differently, and eat different foods. . . . So, I sit down, close my eyes, and open my mind . . . "

—from *Kofi and His Magic* by Maya Angelou, photographs by Margaret Courtney-Clarke

As we commemorate the second anniversary of 9/11, let's remember the children. Kofi, the boy in Maya Angelou's wonderful children's volume, is the epitome of a youngster whose mental horizons have been expanded by books. Whether the tragic events of that awful day two years ago are a horrible lingering image

SEPTEMBER 8 - 14

11 Thursday

PATRIOT DAY

8

9

10

11

12

1

2

3

4

5

6

12 Friday

Jesse Owens born 1913
Barry White born 1944

8

9

10

11

12

1

2

3

4

5

6

13 Saturday

Alain Locke born 1886
Iyanla Vanzant born 1953
Tavis Smiley born 1964
Michael Johnson born 1967

14 Sunday

or a distant bit of television history to the children in your life, books can help you heal, calm, and instruct them about what occurred. Books can also shape our children's reflections, encouraging insight without instilling fear or acrimony.

Much will appear in the media surrounding this sad anniversary, and we will want to be circumspect in what we allow children to view and hear on television and radio. Books can be chosen carefully in advance and shared in intimacy with the fullest possible communication.

Children's book authors are to be applauded for helping us make even the most sensitive subjects accessible to the minds of our very young. Like Kofi, they want to go places, but they often have to travel mental terrain we would rather spare them. Authors for young readers have mapped out both the rough and smooth paths for us.

SEPTEMBER						
S	M	T	W	T	F	S
	1	2	3	4	5	6
7	8	9	10	11	12	13
14	15	16	17	18	19	20
21	22	23	24	25	26	27
28	29	30				

OCTOBER						
S	M	T	W	T	F	S
			1	2	3	4
5	6	7	8	9	10	11
12	13	14	15	16	17	18
19	20	21	22	23	24	25
26	27	28	29	30	31	

SEPTEMBER 2003

15 Monday

Jan Ernst Matzeliger born 1852
Claude McKay born 1889
Anne Moody born 1940
Jessye Norman born 1945

8
9
10
11
12
1
2
3
4
5
6

16 Tuesday

Mamie Smith born 1883
B. B. King born 1925
James Alan McPherson born 1943
Henry Louis Gates, Jr. born 1950

8
9
10
11
12
1
2
3
4
5
6

17 Wednesday

Rube Foster born 1879

8
9
10
11
12
1
2
3
4
5
6

"**If he learns** to read the Bible it will forever unfit him to be a slave. He should know nothing but the will of his master, and learn to obey it. . . . learning will do him no good, but a great deal of harm, making him disconsolate and unhappy."

—Frederick Douglass,
recalling the words of his former master,
from Douglass's autobiography

The African-American heritage of education dates back to the arrival of the first enslaved Africans in America, and reading has been a critical element of the tradition of self-education. The Bible, still the all-time best-selling book, was often the only book available. It became the reading tutor for the enslaved who dared to exercise control of their minds and it offered lessons in the equality of all people in the eyes of God.

SEPTEMBER 15 - 21

18 Thursday
Anna Deavere Smith born 1950

8

9

10

11

12

1

2

3

4

5

6

19 Friday

8

9

10

11

12

1

2

3

4

5

6

20 Saturday
Piri Thomas born 1928

21 Sunday

Literacy was a hard-fought battle. During slavery, being caught reading could mean a life-threatening beating, being maimed, or even the penalty of death.

The anti-literacy rationale by the warped minds who condoned or tolerated slavery was actually based in truth: literacy is power. While no enslaved person could be content and happy in that condition, one who could read had access to power to do something about it. Reading was and remains the basic currency of upward movement in society. From literacy sprung the ability to move in the world beyond the plantation—read signs, gather information from newspapers, make business transactions.

But as important as the practical implications of literacy were its internal benefits. Enslaved African Americans who learned to read broke their own mental shackles.

Mate masie, meaning "I have kept what I have heard," symbolizing wisdom and knowledge

SEPTEMBER						
S	M	T	W	T	F	S
	1	2	3	4	5	6
7	8	9	10	11	12	13
14	15	16	17	18	19	20
21	22	23	24	25	26	27
28	29	30				

OCTOBER						
S	M	T	W	T	F	S
			1	2	3	4
5	6	7	8	9	10	11
12	13	14	15	16	17	18
19	20	21	22	23	24	25
26	27	28	29	30	31	

SEPTEMBER 2003

22 Monday

8

9

10

11

12

1

2

3

4

5

6

23 Tuesday

AUTUMNAL EQUINOX
Mary Church Terrell born 1863
John Coltrane born 1926
Ray Charles born 1930

8

9

10

11

12

1

2

3

4

5

6

24 Wednesday

Frances E. W. Harper born 1825
E. Franklin Frazier born 1894

8

9

10

11

12

1

2

3

4

5

6

"**NEVER** before in the history of the world has a group of people met with such overwhelming challenges and opposition to obtain . . . a higher education. Never before have the odds been so insurmountable, but overcome. At the close of the Civil War, practically all of black America was illiterate; however, by the end of 1910, only 30 percent were. . . . [because] black America saw the rise of a group of schools, colleges, and universities dedicated to providing education to the once servile group."

—Rodney T. Cohen
from *The Black Colleges of Atlanta*

Almost 40% of this country's black graduates were educated at the 105 historically black colleges and universities (HBCUs). HBCUs produce the lion's share of black professionals:

SEPTEMBER 22 - 28

25 Thursday
ROSH HASHANAH BEGINS AT
SUNDOWN
Bell Hooks born 1952

8
9
10
11
12
1
2
3
4
5
6

26 Friday
Serena Williams born 1981

8
9
10
11
12
1
2
3
4
5
6

27 Saturday
Bud Powell born 1924

28 Sunday
David Walker born 1785

Christine's 13th Birthday

75% of black Ph.D.'s
46% of black business executives
50% of black engineers
80% of black federal judges
85% of black doctors
50% of black attorneys
75% of black military officers
40% of black dentists
50% of black pharmacists
75% of black veterinarians

They have also given us many of our favorite writers and book lovers, including Oprah Winfrey, Toni Morrison, and E. Lynn Harris to name just a few. As the school year gets well underway, let's salute these institutions for their heroic work and make sure they thrive to produce the next generation of distinguished African Americans.

SEPTEMBER						
S	M	T	W	T	F	S
	1	2	3	4	5	6
7	8	9	10	11	12	13
14	15	16	17	18	19	20
21	22	23	24	25	26	27
28	29	30				

OCTOBER						
S	M	T	W	T	F	S
			1	2	3	4
5	6	7	8	9	10	11
12	13	14	15	16	17	18
19	20	21	22	23	24	25
26	27	28	29	30	31	

SEPTEMBER – OCTOBER 2003

29 Monday

8
9
10
11
12
1
2
3
4
5
6

30 Tuesday

Cholly Atkins born 1913
Johnny Mathis born 1935
Marilyn McCoo born 1943

8
9
10
11
12
1
2
3
4
5
6

1 Wednesday

8
9
10
11
12
1
2
3
4
5
6

"**For years, black entrepreneurs** have been told that if they want to be successful, they have to wear pinstripes and earn M.B.A.'s. Russell Simmons built his empire on his *own* terms. Often compared by the media to Berry Gordy, of Motown fame, Simmons says he patterns his corporate approach more after David Geffen, the . . . music mogul who adopts a play-by-his-own-rules mentality . . . "

—Derek T. Dingle
from *Black Enterprise: Titans of the B.E. 100s:
Black CEOs Who Redefined and Conquered American Business*

SEPTEMBER 29 - OCTOBER 5

2 Thursday

Nat Turner born 1800
Mahatma Gandhi born 1869

8

9

10

11

12

1

2

3

4

5

6

3 Friday

T. Thomas Fortune born 1856
Chubby Checker born 1941

8

9

10

11

12

1

2

3

4

5

6

4 Saturday

Bernice Johnson Reagon born 1942

5 Sunday

YOM KIPPUR BEGINS AT
SUNDOWN
Autherine Lucy Foster born 1929

Rush is the entertainment company Russell Simmons built to exploit hip-hop culture. Garnering 9-digit dollars annually, Rush is atop the growing list of enterprises founded by black business owners, who have owned and operated businesses since Africans arrived in America. That establishments were held by free blacks in the North and even in the South during the era of slavery, and that there was a brief entrepreneurial flowering of newly emancipated black people during Reconstruction—before the era of lynching and Jim Crow attempted to crush it—are oft-forgotten parts of black history.

Today's black businesses, like so much of American commerce, are frequently service-, information-, or entertainment-based, but historically, black culture has formed much of the foundation for successful African-American companies. Motown was the flagship company for the previous generation, Rush for the current generation.

For book lovers, the current renaissance of black writing and publishing promises the emergence of similar enterprises that will exploit black literary culture. Already self-published authors have stormed the literary gates, and large black-owned publishing houses could soon be on the horizon.

OCTOBER						
S	M	T	W	T	F	S
			1	2	3	4
5	6	7	8	9	10	11
12	13	14	15	16	17	18
19	20	21	22	23	24	25
26	27	28	29	30	31	

NOVEMBER						
S	M	T	W	T	F	S
						1
2	3	4	5	6	7	8
9	10	11	12	13	14	15
16	17	18	19	20	21	22
23/30	24	25	26	27	28	29

OCTOBER 2003

6 Monday
Fannie Lou Hamer born 1917

7 Tuesday
Desmond Tutu born 1931
Amiri Baraka born 1934

8 Wednesday
Faith Ringgold born 1930
Jesse Jackson born 1941

6 Monday	7 Tuesday	8 Wednesday
8	8	8
9	9	9
10	10	10
11	11	11
12	12	12
1	1	1
2	2	2
3	3	3
4	4	4
5	5	5
6	6	6

"The wind came back with triple fury, and put out the light for the last time. They sat in company with the others in other shanties, their eyes straining against crude walls and their souls asking if He meant to measure their puny might against His. They seemed to be staring at the dark, but their eyes were watching God."

—from *Their Eyes Were Watching God*
by Zora Neale Hurston

OCTOBER 6 - 12

9 Thursday

8 _____

9 _____

10 _____

11 _____

12 _____

1 _____

2 _____

3 _____

4 _____

5 _____

6 _____

10 Friday

Frederick Douglass Patterson born 1901
Ben Vereen born 1946
Thelonious Monk born 1917

8 _____

9 _____

10 _____

11 _____

12 _____

1 _____

2 _____

3 _____

4 _____

5 _____

6 _____

11 Saturday

_____

_____

_____

_____

_____

12 Sunday

Ann Petry born 1908
Alice Childress born 1920?
Dick Gregory born 1932

_____

_____

_____

_____

All avid readers have their most beloved authors, favorite books, and remembered passages—or "comfort lines."

Like comfort foods, those dishes to which we turn to build up our weakened emotions, comfort lines nourish hungry minds and souls. And also like comfort foods, comfort lines vary more widely than anyone can imagine, simply due to individual taste.

Mashed yams whipped with heavy cream, hot buttermilk biscuits running with home-made peach preserves, rum raisin ice cream, a plate of collards with a splash of vinegar, a jar of gristly pig feet, grilled tofu with hot sauce—all delectable to someone because they do something magical to her saliva and spoon her memories of joy.

Zora, Alice, Toni (both Morrison and Bambara), Bebe, Terry—each provides her own flavor of comfort lines for the mind. Let's go back to our favorite books and jot down our beloved passages—our personal comfort lines—and when we feel the need, let our minds chew on them.

OCTOBER

S	M	T	W	T	F	S
			1	2	3	4
5	6	7	8	9	10	11
12	13	14	15	16	17	18
19	20	21	22	23	24	25
26	27	28	29	30	31	

NOVEMBER

S	M	T	W	T	F	S
						1
2	3	4	5	6	7	8
9	10	11	12	13	14	15
16	17	18	19	20	21	22
23/30	24	25	26	27	28	29

OCTOBER 2003

13 Monday
COLUMBUS DAY
Arna Bontemps born 1902
Ray Brown born 1926

8

9

10

11

12

1

2

3

4

5

6

14 Tuesday
Oscar Charleston born 1896
Donna Grant born 1956

8

9

10

11

12

1

2

3

4

5

6

15 Wednesday

8

9

10

11

12

1

2

3

4

5

6

"I know it's time for young heads to work toward true illumination. But that bright glare might spotlight a positive HIV test, a lot of time between jobs, the barrel of that gun now loaded, out of the closet, the shoebox tossed. Better to focus on the dim past as we stand on the community steps, peer into a situation where the streetlights still burned bright."

—Eisa Nefertari Ulen
from "What Happened to Your Generation's Promise of
'Love and Revolution'?: A Letter to Angela Davis"

OCTOBER 13 - 19

16 Thursday

8

9

10

11

12

1

2

3

4

5

6

17 Friday

Samuel Ringgold Ward born 1817
Mae Jemison born 1956

8

9

10

11

12

1

2

3

4

5

6

18 Saturday

Chuck Berry born 1926
Ntozake Shange born 1948
Terry McMillan born 1951
Wynton Marsalis born 1961

19 Sunday

Johnnetta Cole born 1936

What makes some writers important is how *uncomfortable* they make us. Now well established in the canon of literature by writers of African descent, Zora Neale Hurston's *Their Eyes Were Watching God* brought discomfort to many of her colleagues when it was published in 1937. This bit of literary history reminds us to abide the discomfort we might feel at reading innovative young writers today.

Such writers are the Hurstons of tomorrow. Their works provoke us to face hard issues, to take seriously the concerns of emerging generations, to relinquish our conceptions of creativity, to give ear to, if not learn to speak, a new literary language. It's important to read them and to let any uneasiness their work arouses serve to instruct us.

OCTOBER						
S	M	T	W	T	F	S
			1	2	3	4
5	6	7	8	9	10	11
12	13	14	15	16	17	18
19	20	21	22	23	24	25
26	27	28	29	30	31	

NOVEMBER						
S	M	T	W	T	F	S
						1
2	3	4	5	6	7	8
9	10	11	12	13	14	15
16	17	18	19	20	21	22
23/30	24	25	26	27	28	29

Se ne tekrema, the teeth and the tongue, a symbol of growth and interdependence

OCTOBER 2003

20 Monday

Ferdinand "Jelly Roll" Morton born 1890?
Fayard Nicholas born 1914

8
9
10
11
12
1
2
3
4
5
6

21 Tuesday

Don Byas born 1912
John Birks "Dizzy" Gillespie born 1917
Florence Ai Ogawa born 1947

8
9
10
11
12
1
2
3
4
5
6

22 Wednesday

Bobby Seale born 1936

8
9
10
11
12
1
2
3
4
5
6

"Sometimes, as the old blues says, Simple might be 'laughing to keep from crying.' But even then, he keeps you laughing, too. If there were not a lot of genial souls in Harlem as talkative as Simple, I would never have these tales to write down that are 'just like him.'"

—Langston Hughes
from the Foreword to *The Best of Simple*

Sometimes we find new, totally current concepts in our old favorite works. Much of Hughes's oeuvre offers us that special gift, not only of timelessness, but constant time*li*ness. His reflections on the everyday challenges of African-American life, made with humor and wit, are as boldly incisive as any statements by today's satirical

OCTOBER 20 - 26

23 Thursday

8 _____

9 _____

10 _____

11 _____

12 _____

1 _____

2 _____

3 _____

4 _____

5 _____

6 _____

24 Friday

Sonny Terry born 1911
Kweisi Mfume born 1948

8 _____

9 _____

10 _____

11 _____

12 _____

1 _____

2 _____

3 _____

4 _____

5 _____

6 _____

25 Saturday

_____

_____

_____

_____

_____

_____

26 Sunday

DAYLIGHT SAVING TIME ENDS
RAMADAN BEGINS
Robert Reed Church, Jr. born 1885
Mahalia Jackson born 1911
Edward Brooke born 1919

_____

_____

_____

_____

---

writers, without being brash and in your face.

Hughes's ability to capture the subtext of black culture is but one of the things that makes his work worth rereading every decade. While the words have remained the same, we, as readers, have changed. We are able to explore the ideas of today, even untangle current issues, in words we have previously read and already savored. Yet somehow, they now offer us fresh meaning.

Our condition as Africans in America has changed dramatically since Hughes penned Simple. Yet Simple remains us. This is so because a great seer wrote among us.

OCTOBER

S	M	T	W	T	F	S
			1	2	3	4
5	6	7	8	9	10	11
12	13	14	15	16	17	18
19	20	21	22	23	24	25
26	27	28	29	30	31	

NOVEMBER

S	M	T	W	T	F	S
						1
2	3	4	5	6	7	8
9	10	11	12	13	14	15
16	17	18	19	20	21	22
23/30	24	25	26	27	28	29

OCTOBER – NOVEMBER 2003

27 Monday

Oliver Tambo born 1917
Ruby Dee born 1924

8

9

10

11

12

1

2

3

4

5

6

28 Tuesday

8

9

10

11

12

1

2

3

4

5

6

29 Wednesday

Melba Moore born 1945

8

9

10

11

12

1

2

3

4

5

6

"Tupac's poems can teach us about universal needs that textbooks rarely address. . . . They also teach us that humanity as a whole suffers if anyone starves. Unfortunately, it took his death to teach us that when one man dies we all bleed."

—Leila Steinberg
from the Introduction to *The Rose That Grew from Concrete*,
by Tupac Shakur

30 Thursday

Clifford Brown born 1930

8

9

10

11

12

1

2

3

4

5

6

31 Friday

HALLOWEEN
Ethel Waters born 1896?

8

9

10

11

12

1

2

3

4

5

6

1 Saturday

Sippie Wallace born 1898

2 Sunday

Michelle Cliff born 1946

The popularity of the poetry of Tupac Shakur is proof that a new generation of artists are forcing their way into African-American verse. Rooted in a style of hip-hop music dubbed "gangsta rap," these writers are taking contemporary poetry by storm, or as they would say, "bum rushing" old poetic forms.

Book lovers can quake and hide, returning to the now-safe places of the Renaissance or Black Arts Movement poets. But more inquisitive minds will remove the dead-bolt and open the door for these new artists, remembering that all the now-classic forms were once brand new experiments.

While new artists need "gangsta" courage to put forth their work, readers also need a radical courage to read, explore, and seek to understand their words.

We will never know what Tupac would have produced, but we can honor his brief life by letting his written work introduce us to a new generation of writers.

OCTOBER

S	M	T	W	T	F	S
			1	2	3	4
5	6	7	8	9	10	11
12	13	14	15	16	17	18
19	20	21	22	23	24	25
26	27	28	29	30	31	

NOVEMBER

S	M	T	W	T	F	S
						1
2	3	4	5	6	7	8
9	10	11	12	13	14	15
16	17	18	19	20	21	22
23/30	24	25	26	27	28	29

NOVEMBER 2003

3 Monday

Lois Mailou Jones born 1905

4 Tuesday

5 Wednesday

8	8	8
9	9	9
10	10	10
11	11	11
12	12	12
1	1	1
2	2	2
3	3	3
4	4	4
5	5	5
6	6	6

"Slave-made cloth was not always crude material fit only for slave use; rather it was on occasion of high enough quality to be used in the 'Big House.' . . . In one case a slave weaver in Bosque County was awarded a prize for her work."

—John Michael Vlach
from *By the Work of Their Hands: Studies in Afro-American Folklife*

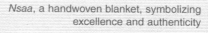

Nsaa, a handwoven blanket, symbolizing excellence and authenticity

NOVEMBER 3 - 9

6 Thursday
Thandie Newton born 1972

8	
9	
10	
11	
12	
1	
2	
3	
4	
5	
6	

7 Friday

8	
9	
10	
11	
12	
1	
2	
3	
4	
5	
6	

8 Saturday
Alfre Woodard born 1953

9 Sunday
Benjamin Banneker born 1731
Dorothy Dandridge born 1922?
Alice Coachman born 1923

The month before Christmas begins the season of gift buying. But it wasn't always so. Until the last few generations, this season in African-American households was marked by gift-*making*. Arts and crafts remain alive and well as hobbies in our communities today, but they were essential to our forebears, especially those who lived during the eras of slavery, Reconstruction, and before the Great Migration to the North.

Despite the condescension—apparent in the quote at left—of often well-meaning scholars who have studied and preserved some of the oldest examples of folk art and handiwork by enslaved Africans in America, such work is rapidly taking its place among the preeminent folk art in the nation. And, as the quote notes, the beauty and skill evident in black arts and crafts have long been awarded respect and recognition, even when its makers were not.

Before being swept into the sea of holiday gift shopping, consider handmade arts and crafts as gifts. Handmade items are not only rich in sentimental value, but cultural value as well. Support African-American craftmakers at fairs and specialty shops, or, even better, dust off those old projects or pick up a do-it-yourself kit and join your own hands to a long, beautiful tradition.

NOVEMBER

S	M	T	W	T	F	S
						1
2	3	4	5	6	7	8
9	10	11	12	13	14	15
16	17	18	19	20	21	22
23/30	24	25	26	27	28	29

DECEMBER

S	M	T	W	T	F	S
	1	2	3	4	5	6
7	8	9	10	11	12	13
14	15	16	17	18	19	20
21	22	23	24	25	26	27
28	29	30	31			

NOVEMBER 2003

10 Monday

8

9

10

11

12

1

2

3

4

5

6

11 Tuesday

VETERANS' DAY
Shirley Graham Du Bois born 1896?

8

9

10

11

12

1

2

3

4

5

6

12 Wednesday

Buck Clayton born 1911

8

9

10

11

12

1

2

3

4

5

6

"The [Vietnam] war, which had bitterly divided America like no other issue since the Civil War, had become a double battleground . . ."

—Wallace Terry
from *Bloods: An Oral History of the Vietnam War by Black Veterans*

NOVEMBER 10 - 16

13 Thursday
James T. Rapier born 1837
Bennie Moten born 1894
Whoopi Goldberg born 1949?

8 _____
9 _____
10 _____
11 _____
12 _____
1 _____
2 _____
3 _____
4 _____
5 _____
6 _____

14 Friday

8 _____
9 _____
10 _____
11 _____
12 _____
1 _____
2 _____
3 _____
4 _____
5 _____
6 _____

15 Saturday

16 Sunday
W. C. Handy born 1873
Chinua Achebe born 1930
Jervey Tervalon born 1958

Veterans' Day is a good opportunity to remember that black men (and recently women) have served in every American war—beginning with the Revolutionary War. But all the wars have been a "double battleground" for African Americans, with a war for equality being waged with our countrymen at the same time as war is fought with the declared—or in the case of Vietnam, undeclared—opponent.

As we observe Veterans' Day, let's be sure to give some special love to the men and women in our lives who have sacrificed for our nation, despite its failing. That deserves a special salute.

As lovers of reading who know the pen is mightier than the sword and the much-borrowed book more ballistic than the air brigade, we honor black veterans while holding the vision of a powerful pacifism learned from reading. For it is books with the stories of war that remind us that wars are never truly won by anyone.

NOVEMBER						
S	M	T	W	T	F	S
						1
2	3	4	5	6	7	8
9	10	11	12	13	14	15
16	17	18	19	20	21	22
23/30	24	25	26	27	28	29

DECEMBER						
S	M	T	W	T	F	S
	1	2	3	4	5	6
7	8	9	10	11	12	13
14	15	16	17	18	19	20
21	22	23	24	25	26	27
28	29	30	31			

NOVEMBER 2003

17 Monday

8
9
10
11
12
1
2
3
4
5
6

18 Tuesday

Howard Thurman born 1900
Tina McElroy Ansa born 1949

8
9
10
11
12
1
2
3
4
5
6

19 Wednesday

Roy Campanella born 1921
Gail Devers born 1966

8
9
10
11
12
1
2
3
4
5
6

"Under no circumstances should you treat your friends with more respect than you do your family. . . . Remembering birthdays, offering assistance during illness, and keeping promises are not reserved for friends."

—Karen Grigsby Bates and Karen Elyse Hudson
from *Basic Black: Home Training for Modern Times*

NOVEMBER 17 - 23

20 Thursday

21 Friday

Coleman Hawkins born 1904

22 Saturday

Guion Stewart Bluford, Jr. born 1942
Valerie Wilson Wesley born 1947

8

9

10

11

12

1

2

3

4

5

6

8

9

10

11

12

1

2

3

4

5

6

23 Sunday

Gayl Jones born 1949

Soup kitchens and other helping programs are deluged with volunteers during the holidays. Friends are invited to our homes and we give parties for our associates. This is and is not as it should be. Yes, we should extend ourselves to the needy and celebrate the people that make our lives full, but as the holiday season approaches, let's reconsider family.

While we love our families, we all sometimes take them for granted. We know they'll understand if we forget, don't have time, or something comes up. Those closest to us are sometimes the most overlooked when it comes to special ways of caring. We get caught in the routine.

The upcoming holidays are a chance for us to break routine and show our family members special consideration, surprising love, and extraordinary care. Let's outdo the best things we did this year for friends with better for our family.

NOVEMBER

S	M	T	W	T	F	S
						1
2	3	4	5	6	7	8
9	10	11	12	13	14	15
16	17	18	19	20	21	22
23/30	24	25	26	27	28	29

DECEMBER

S	M	T	W	T	F	S
	1	2	3	4	5	6
7	8	9	10	11	12	13
14	15	16	17	18	19	20
21	22	23	24	25	26	27
28	29	30	31			

NOVEMBER 2003

24 Monday
Scott Joplin born 1868

25 Tuesday

26 Wednesday
Tina Turner born 1939

24 Monday	25 Tuesday	26 Wednesday
8	8	8
9	9	9
10	10	10
11	11	11
12	12	12
1	1	1
2	2	2
3	3	3
4	4	4
5	5	5
6	6	6

"**When I was 7 years old,** my grandmother started teaching me how to cook. We had 12 people in our family and she needed all the help she could get!

I was so small she gave me my own special stool to help me reach the table. I remember standing on that stool trying to roll out biscuit dough that was so big I could never do it by myself. I would try so hard but only end up with flour everywhere! I'll never forget how grandma would come over, put her arm around my shoulders and say, 'It's all right, sugar, you'll be big enough some day.' She never got upset with me for being too small. Every time I make biscuits I remember those early days with my grandmother. And even though I'm big enough now to roll out the dough by myself, I can still feel grandma stand-ing next to me . . . helping me."

—Pearletha Nelson
from *The Black Family Reunion Cookbook: Recipes and Food Memories*

NOVEMBER 24 - 30

27 Thursday
THANKSGIVING
Jimi Hendrix born 1942

28 Friday
Dennis Brutus born 1924
Berry Gordy, Jr. born 1929

29 Saturday
Adam Clayton Powell, Jr. born 1908
Billy Strayhorn born 1915
Pearl Primus born 1919

8

9

10

11

12

1

2

3

4

5

6

30 Sunday
FIRST SUNDAY IN ADVENT
Gordon Parks, Sr. born 1912
Shirley Chisholm born 1924

If Thanksgiving for your family means more time spent watching TV than talking; more listening to music than to spouse, parent, or children; more time on the Internet than interacting with others, you may need to learn new ways to relate intimately, in this age when most relating is electronic.

In the midst of increasing affluence in Black America, we need most to make Thanksgiving a time of heartfelt and expressed interactions, rather than a food orgy accompanied by sports channels. This is not as simple as turning off the TV, CD player, or play station or dragging little sister's head out of that romance novel. Deepened relationships can't be forced or coerced. People must be drawn into new ways of interacting and experience them as immensely pleasurable.

But, old ways can yield powerful new results. Start in the kitchen, by sharing the cooking. Assign everyone a meal preparation task, and work in teams. The kitchen may end up messier and the food may not be quite as flavorful, but everyone will be able to taste the love.

NOVEMBER
S	M	T	W	T	F	S
						1
2	3	4	5	6	7	8
9	10	11	12	13	14	15
16	17	18	19	20	21	22
23/30	24	25	26	27	28	29

DECEMBER
S	M	T	W	T	F	S
	1	2	3	4	5	6
7	8	9	10	11	12	13
14	15	16	17	18	19	20
21	22	23	24	25	26	27
28	29	30	31			

DECEMBER 2003

1 Monday
Rosa Parks arrested for refusing to move to the back of the bus 1955

8
9
10
11
12
1
2
3
4
5
6

2 Tuesday
Harry Thacker Burleigh born 1866

8
9
10
11
12
1
2
3
4
5
6

3 Wednesday

8
9
10
11
12
1
2
3
4
5
6

"From the time I can first recall the rain falling on the red clay in Florida, I wanted to make things. When my brothers and sisters were making mud pies, I would be making ducks and chickens with the mud."

—Augusta Savage
from *Black Women in America: An Historical Encyclopedia*

Sculptor Augusta Savage lived from 1892 until 1962, and produced an immensely popular sculpture for the 1939 World's Fair. Though little of Savage's body of work survives, her simple words inspire us to follow

DECEMBER 1 - 7

4 Thursday

Tyra Banks born 1973

8

9

10

11

12

1

2

3

4

5

6

5 Friday

Little Richard (Penniman) born 1935?

8

9

10

11

12

1

2

3

4

5

6

6 Saturday

7 Sunday

Gordon Parks, Jr. born 1934
Pearl Cleage born 1948

---

our own creative visions, to encourage artistic urges in others, and to support black visual artists.

This holiday season will be marked by massive numbers of "black" images—on cards and wrappings, in the media, and as gifts. Let's note whether these images reflect the African-American experience with dignity and make the extra effort required to seek out and buy visual material created by black artists.

Just to be selected to create a monumental work was an awesome accomplishment for Savage, since her time was marked by the rise of Hitler in Europe and the rule of Jim Crow segregation and oppression in the United States. But Savage never received her due. Let's ensure that Savage's "children"—today's visual artists—are celebrated and that their work endures.

DECEMBER						
S	M	T	W	T	F	S
	1	2	3	4	5	6
7	8	9	10	11	12	13
14	15	16	17	18	19	20
21	22	23	24	25	26	27
28	29	30	31			

JANUARY						
S	M	T	W	T	F	S
				1	2	3
4	5	6	7	8	9	10
11	12	13	14	15	16	17
18	19	20	21	22	23	24
25	26	27	28	29	30	31

DECEMBER 2003

8 Monday
Sammy Davis, Jr. born 1925

8

9

10

11

12

1

2

3

4

5

6

9 Tuesday
Roy DeCarava born 1919

8

9

10

11

12

1

2

3

4

5

6

10 Wednesday
Ralph Bunche awarded Nobel Peace Prize 1950

8

9

10

11

12

1

2

3

4

5

6

"We made Christmas very special by getting together at my grand-mother's house. On Christmas Day, we loved to sit down and eat a big meal with all the trimmings. The best part was all the talking we did. . . . Great conversation was as sweet and rich as any holiday dessert. I believe that Christmas is about enjoying what you have. . . ."

—Omar Epps, as told to Allison Samuels, from *Christmas Soul: African American Holiday Stories*

Odo nyera fie kwan, "Love does not get lost on its way home," a symbol of love, devotion, and faithfulness

DECEMBER 8 - 14

11 Thursday

8

9

10

11

12

1

2

3

4

5

6

12 Friday

Dionne Warwick born 1940?

8

9

10

11

12

1

2

3

4

5

6

13 Saturday

14 Sunday

John Mercer Langston born 1829
Stanley Crouch born 1945

Getting into the Christmas spirit is putting the meaning before the shopping, decorating, cooking, and partying. Instead of counting down the days and eyeing the "to do" list, let's follow Omar Epps's lead and enjoy what we have.

We can start by taking a Christmas inventory, rather than making a Christmas list.

Let's begin with a people inventory. Who makes up your family—spouse, children, parents, other blood kin? What about your friends—who are your staples (close, long-term homies); your occasional treats (buddies in other cities); specialty goods (office mates, church fellows, sorority sisters)? There's much to enjoy about the people in our lives.

Next let's do a self inventory. What about our health, emotional equilibrium, mental acuity, fitness? It's a joy being alive.

If we never took an inventory of our material possessions, there would already be plenty "of what we have" to enjoy this Christmas and many more.

DECEMBER						
S	M	T	W	T	F	S
	1	2	3	4	5	6
7	8	9	10	11	12	13
14	15	16	17	18	19	20
21	22	23	24	25	26	27
28	29	30	31			

JANUARY						
S	M	T	W	T	F	S
				1	2	3
4	5	6	7	8	9	10
11	12	13	14	15	16	17
18	19	20	21	22	23	24
25	26	27	28	29	30	31

DECEMBER 2003

15 Monday

16 Tuesday

17 Wednesday

Deborah Sampson born 1760
Sy Oliver born 1910

15 Monday	16 Tuesday	17 Wednesday
8	8	8
9	9	9
10	10	10
11	11	11
12	12	12
1	1	1
2	2	2
3	3	3
4	4	4
5	5	5
6	6	6

"THERE ARE AT LEAST FIVE COMMON SETS OF VALUES AND PRACTICES CENTRAL TO AFRICAN FIRST FRUIT CELEBRATIONS WHICH INFORMED THE DEVELOPMENT OF KWANZAA: INGATHERING, REVERENCE, COMMEMORATION, RECOMMITMENT, AND CELEBRATION."

—MAULANA KARENGA, FOUNDER OF KWANZAA, FROM *THE AFRICAN AMERICAN HOLIDAY OF KWANZAA: A CELEBRATION OF FAMILY, COMMUNITY AND CULTURE*

Established thirty-seven years ago as a cultural celebration of our African roots, Kwanzaa has become a vibrant ritual in Black America, reminiscent of the African "first fruits" observances from which its Swahili name derives.

Beginning the day after Christmas—Kwanzaa is not a religious, but a cultural celebration—seven principles,

DECEMBER 15 - 21

18 Thursday

Proclamation made of the ratification of
    the 13TH Amendment 1865
Benjamin O. Davis, Jr. born 1912
Ossie Davis born 1917

8

9

10

11

12

1

2

3

4

5

6

19 Friday

HANUKKAH BEGINS AT
    SUNDOWN
Carter G. Woodson born 1875
Cicely Tyson born 1933

8

9

10

11

12

1

2

3

4

5

6

20 Saturday

William Julius Wilson born 1935

21 Sunday

Josh Gibson born 1911
Florence Griffith Joyner born 1959

---

collectively named the *Nguzo Saba*, are each formally assigned a day:

    Umoja, unity
    Kujichagulia, self-determination
    Ujima, collective work and responsibility
    Ujamaa, cooperative economics
    Nia, purpose
    Kuumba, creativity
    Imani, faith

Plan ahead to close out the year and bring in the new with meaningful celebrations of these common-sense cultural values rather than with champagne and party hats.

DECEMBER

S	M	T	W	T	F	S
	1	2	3	4	5	6
7	8	9	10	11	12	13
14	15	16	17	18	19	20
21	22	23	24	25	26	27
28	29	30	31			

JANUARY

S	M	T	W	T	F	S
				1	2	3
4	5	6	7	8	9	10
11	12	13	14	15	16	17
18	19	20	21	22	23	24
25	26	27	28	29	30	31

DECEMBER 2003

22 Monday
WINTER SOLSTICE
Jean-Michel Basquiat born 1960

8

9

10

11

12

1

2

3

4

5

6

23 Tuesday
Sarah Breedlove Walker born 1867

8

9

10

11

12

1

2

3

4

5

6

24 Wednesday
Warren Dodds born 1898

8

9

10

11

12

1

2

3

4

5

6

"We watch proudly as our youth excel in city or statewide exams; we beam at those who at year's end throw their mortar boards high in the air–graduates of some fine institution of learning; we stand in the wings as we see our young people become lawyers, sanitation workers, entrepreneurs, carpenters, teachers, secretaries, nurses, construction workers, army personnel, loving home-makers, professional athletes, historians. Like the village elders, we pat our chests because we know it takes a village to raise a child."

—Maxine M. Walker
from *Holy Bible: The African American Jubilee Edition*

DECEMBER 22 - 28

25 Thursday

CHRISTMAS
Cab Calloway born 1907

8 _____

9 _____

10 _____

11 _____

12 _____

1 _____

2 _____

3 _____

4 _____

5 _____

6 _____

26 Friday

1ST DAY OF KWANZAA:
  UMOJA (UNITY)
Jean Toomer born 1894

8 _____

9 _____

10 _____

11 _____

12 _____

1 _____

2 _____

3 _____

4 _____

5 _____

6 _____

27 Saturday

2ND DAY OF KWANZAA:
  KUJICHAGULIA
  (SELF-DETERMINATION)

28 Sunday

3RD DAY OF KWANZAA:
  UJIMA (COLLECTIVE WORK
  AND RESPONSIBILITY)
Earl "Fatha" Hines born 1903
Denzel Washington born 1954

As the sun sets on one year and we look forward to the dawn of another, it's good to savor the recent sweet memories and digest the lessons learned from bitter ones. Ultimately, it's all good, the bitter and the sweet.

In the same way that it takes all kinds of personalities to make up this amorphous, yet very real community—or village—that we call African America, it takes a full range of experiences to make us each a beautiful community of one.

Let's march, with the blessings and challenges of this year like a boot on each foot, into the New Year, shoulder to shoulder in diverse unity with our entire village.

DECEMBER

S	M	T	W	T	F	S
	1	2	3	4	5	6
7	8	9	10	11	12	13
14	15	16	17	18	19	20
21	22	23	24	25	26	27
28	29	30	31			

JANUARY

S	M	T	W	T	F	S
				1	2	3
4	5	6	7	8	9	10
11	12	13	14	15	16	17
18	19	20	21	22	23	24
25	26	27	28	29	30	31

DECEMBER 2003 - JANUARY 2004

29 Monday

4TH DAY OF KWANZAA:
UJAMAA (COOPERATIVE
ECONOMICS)

Robert Clifton Weaver born 1907

8 _____
9 _____
10 _____
11 _____
12 _____
1 _____
2 _____
3 _____
4 _____
5 _____
6 _____

30 Tuesday

5TH DAY OF KWANZAA: NIA
(PURPOSE)

8 _____
9 _____
10 _____
11 _____
12 _____
1 _____
2 _____
3 _____
4 _____
5 _____
6 _____

31 Wednesday

NEW YEAR'S EVE
6TH DAY OF KWANZAA: KUUMBA
(CREATIVITY)

Odetta born 1930

8 _____
9 _____
10 _____
11 _____
12 _____
1 _____
2 _____
3 _____
4 _____
5 _____
6 _____

"Sing a song full of the faith that the
dark past has taught us,
Sing a song full of the hope that the
present has brought us;
Facing the rising sun of our new day begun,
Let us march on till victory is won."

—From "Lift Every Voice and Sing"
by James Weldon Johnson

Nyame biribi wo soro, symbol of hope and aspiration. *"Nyame biribi wo soro na ma mensa nka,"* meaning "God, there is something in the heavens, let me reach it."

DECEMBER 29 – JANUARY 4

1 Thursday

NEW YEAR'S DAY
7TH DAY OF KWANZAA: IMANI
   (FAITH)

8

9

10

11

12

1

2

3

4

5

6

2 Friday

Oscar Micheaux born 1884
E. Simms Campbell born 1906
John Hope Franklin born 1915

8

9

10

11

12

1

2

3

4

5

6

3 Saturday

Alonzo J. Ransier born 1834
Herbie Nichols born 1919

4 Sunday

Nancy Mendes

DECEMBER						
S	M	T	W	T	F	S
	1	2	3	4	5	6
7	8	9	10	11	12	13
14	15	16	17	18	19	20
21	22	23	24	25	26	27
28	29	30	31			

JANUARY						
S	M	T	W	T	F	S
				1	2	3
4	5	6	7	8	9	10
11	12	13	14	15	16	17
18	19	20	21	22	23	24
25	26	27	28	29	30	31

2004 Planner

JANUARY

SUN	MON	TUE	WED	THU	FRI	SAT
				1	2	3
4	5	6	7	8	9	10
11	12	13	14	15	16	17
18	19	20	21	22	23	24
25	26	27	28	29	30	31

FEBRUARY

SUN	MON	TUE	WED	THU	FRI	SAT
1	2	3	4	5	6	7
8	9	10	11	12	13	14
15	16	17	18	19	20	21
22	23	24	25	26	27	28
29						

MARCH

SUN	MON	TUE	WED	THU	FRI	SAT
	1	2	3	4	5	6
7	8	9	10	11	12	13
14	15	16	17	18	19	20
21	22	23	24	25	26	27
28	29	30	31			

2004 Planner

APRIL

SUN	MON	TUE	WED	THU	FRI	SAT
				1	2	3
4	5	6	7	8	9	10
11	12	13	14	15	16	17
18	19	20	21	22	23	24
25	26	27	28	29	30	

MAY

SUN	MON	TUE	WED	THU	FRI	SAT
						1
2	3	4	5	6	7	8
9	10	11	12	13	14	15
16	17	18	19	20	21	22
$^{23}/_{30}$	$^{24}/_{31}$	25	26	27	28	29

JUNE

SUN	MON	TUE	WED	THU	FRI	SAT
		1	2	3	4	5
6	7	8	9	10	11	12
13	14	15	16	17	18	19
20	21	22	23	24	25	26
27	28	29	30			

2004 Planner

JULY

SUN	MON	TUE	WED	THU	FRI	SAT
				1	2	3
4	5	6	7	8	9	10
11	12	13	14	15	16	17
18	19	20	21	22	23	24
25	26	27	28	29	30	31

AUGUST

SUN	MON	TUE	WED	THU	FRI	SAT
1	2	3	4	5	6	7
8	9	10	11	12	13	14
15	16	17	18	19	20	21
22	23	24	25	26	27	28
29	30	31				

SEPTEMBER

SUN	MON	TUE	WED	THU	FRI	SAT
			1	2	3	4
5	6	7	8	9	10	11
12	13	14	15	16	17	18
19	20	21	22	23	24	25
26	27	28	29	30		

2004 Planner

OCTOBER

SUN	MON	TUE	WED	THU	FRI	SAT
					1	2
3	4	5	6	7	8	9
10	11	12	13	14	15	16
17	18	19	20	21	22	23
24/31	25	26	27	28	29	30

NOVEMBER

SUN	MON	TUE	WED	THU	FRI	SAT
	1	2	3	4	5	6
7	8	9	10	11	12	13
14	15	16	17	18	19	20
21	22	23	24	25	26	27
28	29	30				

DECEMBER

SUN	MON	TUE	WED	THU	FRI	SAT
			1	2	3	4
5	6	7	8	9	10	11
12	13	14	15	16	17	18
19	20	21	22	23	24	25
26	27	28	29	30	31	

Toll-Free Numbers
and Websites

CREDIT CARDS (LOST OR STOLEN)

AMERICAN EXPRESS www.americanexpress.com
- USA 800-528-4800
- Canada 800-263-9222

MASTERCARD www.mastercard.com
- USA & Canada 800-307-7309

VISA www.visa.com
- USA & Canada 800-847-2911

U.S. AIRLINES

American www.americanairlines.com 800-433-7300
America West www.americawest.com 800-235-9292
Continental www.continental.com 800-525-0280
Delta www.delta.com 800-221-1212
Northwest www.nwa.com 800-225-2525
United www.united.com 800-241-6522
USAirways www.usairways.com 800-428-4322

INTERNATIONAL AIRLINES

Aero Mexico www.aeromexico.com 800-237-6639
Air Canada www.aircanada.ca 888-247-2262
Air Jamaica www.airjamaica.com 800-523-5585
British Airways www.british-airways.com 800-247-9297
Finnair www.finnair.com 800-950-5000
Iberia Airlines www.iberia.com 800-772-4642
Icelandair www.icelandair.is 800-223-5500
Japan Air Lines www.japanair.com 800-525-3663
KLM www.klm.nl 800-374-7747
Korean Air www.koreanair.com 800-438-5000
Lufthansa www.lufthansa.com 800-645-3880
Qantas Airways www.qantas.com 800-227-4500
South African Airways www.flysaa.com 800-722-9675
Swiss www.swiss.com 877-359-7947
Virgin Atlantic www.virgin-atlantic.com 800-862-8621

AUTOMOBILE RENTALS

Alamo Rent-A-Car www.alamo.com 800-327-9633
Avis Rent-A-Car www.avis.com 800-331-1212
Budget Rent-A-Car www.budget.com 800-527-0700
Dollar Rent-A-Car www.dollar.com 800-800-4000
Hertz Rent-A-Car www.hertz.com 800-654-3131
National Car Rental www.nationalcar.com 800-CAR-RENT
Thrifty Car Rental www.thrifty.com 800-367-2277

HOTELS AND MOTELS

Best Western Motels www.bestwestern.com 800-528-1234
Comfort Inns www.comfortinn.com 800-424-6423
Days Inns www.daysinn.com 800-329-7466
Doubletree Hotels www.doubletree.com 800-222-8733
Econo Lodges www.econolodge.com 877-424-6423
Embassy Suites www.embassysuites.com 800-EMBASSY
Fiesta Americana www.fiestaamericana.com 800-FIESTA-1
Hampton Inns www.hampton-inn.com 800-HAMPTON
Hilton Hotels www.hilton.com 800-445-8667
Holiday Inns www.6c.com 800-465-4329
Hotel InterContinental www.interconti.com 800-327-0200
Howard Johnson www.hojo.com 800-654-2000
Hyatt Hotels www.hyatt.com 800-233-1234
Marriott Hotels www.marriott.com 800-228-9290
Radisson Hotels www.radisson.com 800-333-3333
Ramada Inns www.ramada.com 800-2RAMADA
Red Carpet Inns www.bookroomsnow.com 800-251-1962
Red Lion Hotels & Inns www.redlion.com 800-547-8010
Renaissance Hotels www.renaissancehotels.com 888-236-2427
Resorts International www.resorts-international.com 800-336-6378
Sheraton Hotels & Inns www.starwood.com 800-325-3535
Sonesta International Hotels www.sonesta.com 800-766-3782
Travel Lodge www.travelodge.com 800-578-7878
Westin Hotels www.starwood.com 800-228-3000

Anniversary Gifts, Birthstones/Flowers, Holidays

ANNIVERSARY GIFTS

YEAR	TRADITIONAL	MODERN
1st	Paper	Clocks
2nd	Cotton	China
3rd	Leather	Crystal, Glass
4th	Books	Appliances
5th	Wood	Silverware
6th	Candy, Iron	Wood
7th	Wool, Copper	Desk Sets
8th	Bronze, Pottery	Linens, Lace
9th	Pottery, Willow	Leather
10th	Tin, Aluminum	Diamond Jewelry
11th	Steel	Fashion Jewelry
12th	Silk, Linen	Pearls
13th	Lace	Textiles, Furs
14th	Ivory	Gold Jewelry
15th	Crystal	Watches
20th	China	Platinum
25th	Silver	Silver
30th	Pearl	Diamond
35th	Coral	Jade
40th	Ruby	Ruby
50th	Gold	Gold
55th	Emerald	Emerald
60th	Diamond	Diamond
75th	Diamond	Diamond

BIRTHSTONES/FLOWERS

MONTH	STONE	FLOWER
January	Garnet	Carnation
February	Amethyst	Violet
March	Bloodstone	Jonquil
April	Diamond	Sweet Pea
May	Emerald	Lily of the Valley
June	Pearl	Rose
July	Ruby	Larkspur
August	Sardonyx	Gladiolus
September	Sapphire	Aster
October	Opal	Calendula
November	Topaz	Chrysanthemum
December	Turquoise	Narcissus

HOLIDAYS 2003

New Year's Day	January 1
Martin Luther King Jr. Day	January 20
Groundhog Day	February 2
Lincoln's Birthday	February 12
Valentine's Day	February 14
Presidents' Day	February 17
Washington's Birthday	February 22
Ash Wednesday	March 5
St. Patrick's Day	March 17
First Day of Spring	March 20
April Fool's Day	April 1
Daylight Saving Time begins	April 6
Palm Sunday	April 13
Passover begins at sundown	April 16
Good Friday	April 18
Easter Sunday	April 20
Earth Day	April 22
National Arbor Day	April 25
Mother's Day	May 11
Armed Forces Day (U.S.)	May 17
Victoria Day (Canada)	May 19
Memorial Day (observed)	May 26
Flag Day	June 14
Father's Day	June 15
First Day of Summer	June 21
Canada Day	July 1
Independence Day (U.S.)	July 4
Labor Day	September 1
First Day of Autumn	September 23
Rosh Hashanah begins at sundown	September 25
Yom Kippur begins at sundown	October 5
Columbus Day (observed)	October 13
Thanksgiving Day (Canada)	October 13
Daylight Saving Time ends	October 26
Ramadan begins	October 26
Halloween	October 31
Veterans' Day	November 11
Thanksgiving Day (U.S.)	November 27
Hanukkah begins at sundown	December 19
First Day of Winter	December 22
Christmas Day	December 25
Boxing Day (Canada)	December 26
Kwanzaa begins	December 26
New Year's Eve	December 31

Notes

6/18 - Recieved the paperwork from I.C. Still they say no operation and no compensation. Went to see Dr. Byrne this morning and he was highly upset about the situation says the surgery needs to happen and who doesn't know that. Blaque was with me he acted like he wasn't to interested but who knows I wonder about him He doesn't seem that interested or maybe its just me.

6/20/03

Blaque had to leave his mother was in an accident someone hit her from behind. Hell he's been gone all day so what to do his father called says there having a cookout and they want us to come we will see. If he doesn't go Becky & I will. At least me will have someone to talk too. My husband is so into everyone else problems he doesn't see anything wrong in his own home. I'm tired of being alone all the time it gets to be depressing

Notes

Notes

Notes

Notes

Sources

12/30/02: "How It Feels to Be Colored Me," by Zora Neale Hurston. First appeared in *The World Tomorrow 11*, May 1928.

1/6/03 and 1/20/03: *Black Heroes*, by Jessie Carney Smith (Visible Ink Press).

1/13/03: *The Autobiography of Martin Luther King, Jr.*, edited by Clayborne Carson (Warner Books, Inc.).

1/27/03: *The Reckoning: What Blacks Owe to Each Other*, by Randall Robinson (Penguin Putnam Inc.).

2/03/03: *The Mis-Education of the Negro*, by Carter G. Woodson, was first published by in 1933.

2/10/03: *Love Poems*, by Nikki Giovanni (William Morrow and Company, Inc.).

2/17/03: *Freedom Days: 365 Inspired Moments in Civil Rights History*, by Janus Adams (John Wiley & Sons, Inc.).

2/24/03 and 8/25/03: *The African-American Century*, by Henry Louis Gates, Jr. and Cornel West (The Free Press, a division of Simon and Schuster, Inc.).

3/3/03: *Sister Strength*, compiled by Rev. Dr. Suzan Johnson Cook (Thomas Nelson, Inc., Publishers).

3/10/03 and 5/12/03: *The Norton Anthology of African American Literature*, Henry Louis Gates, Jr. and Nellie Y. McKay, General Editors (W. W. Norton & Company, Inc.).

3/17/03: *Powerful Black Women* by Jessie Carney Smith (Visible Ink Press).

3/24/03: *Leontyne Price: Highlights of a Prima Donna*, by Hugh Lee Lyon (Vantage Press, Inc.).

3/31/03: *An African Prayer Book*, by Desmond Tutu (Bantam Doubleday Dell Publishing Group, Inc.).

4/7/03: *Fire in His Heart: Bishop Benjamin Tucker Tanner and the A.M.E. Church*, by William Seraile, (The University of Tennessee Press).

4/14/03 and 12/22/03: *Holy Bible: The African American Jubilee Edition* (American Bible Society).

4/21/03: *Sepia Dreams: A Celebration of Black Achievement Through Words and Images*, by Matthew Jordan Smith and Dionne Bennett (St. Martin's Press).

4/28/03: *Ev'ry Time I Feel the Spirit: 101 Best-Loved Psalms, Hymns, and Spiritual Songs of the African-American Church* by Gwendolin Sims Warren (Henry Holt and Company, Inc.).

5/5/03: *Beloved*, by Toni Morrison (Alfred A. Knopf, Inc.).

5/19/03: *The Autobiography of Malcolm X*, by Malcolm X with the assistance of Alex Haley (Ballantine Books).

5/26/03: *The Life of Langston Hughes* by Arnold Rampersad (Oxford University Press).

6/2/03: *Singing in the Comeback Choir*, by Bebe Moore Campbell (Penguin Putnam, Inc.).

6/9/03: *Boys into Men: Raising Our African American Teenage Sons*, by Nancy Boyd-Franklin, Ph.D. and A. J. Franklin, Ph.D. with Pamela A. Toussaint (The Penguin Group).

6/16/03: *My American Journey*, by Colin L. Powell with Joseph E. Persico (Random House, Inc.).

6/23/03: *Cosbyology*, by William H. Cosby Jr. (Hyperion).

6/30/03: *Incidents in the Life of a Slave Girl*, by Linda Brent (pseudonym for Harriet Jacobs), was first published in 1861.

7/7/03: *Lest We Forget: The Passage from Africa to Slavery and Emancipation*, by Velma Maia Thomas (Crown Publishers, Inc.).

7/14/03: *Black Song: The Forge and the Flame: The Story of How the Afro-American Spiritual was Hammered Out*, by John Lovell, Jr. (Macmillan Company).

7/21/03: *Black Jacks: African American Seamen in the Age of Sail*, by W. Jeffrey Bolster (Harvard University Press).

7/28/03: *Freedom's Children: The Passage from Emancipation to the Great Migration* by Velma Maia Thomas, (Crown).

8/4/03 and 11/24/03: *The Black Family Reunion Cookbook: Recipes and Food Memories*, from The National Council of Negro Women (Fireside).

8/11/03: *Wearing Purple*, by Lydia Lewis Alexander, Marilyn Hill Harper, Otis Holloway Owens, Mildred Lucas Patterson (Crown Publishers).

8/18/03: *The Divine Nine: The History of African American Fraternities and Sororities*, by Lawrence C. Ross, Jr. (Kensington Publishing Corp.).

9/1/03: *Up From Slavery: The Autobiography of Booker T. Washington* was first published in 1901.

9/8/03: *Kofi and His Magic*, by Maya Angelou, photographs by Margaret Courtney-Clarke (Clarkson N. Potter Publishers).

9/15/03: *Life and Times of Frederick Douglass* by Frederick Douglass was first pubished in 1881 and revised in 1892.

9/22/03: *The Black Colleges of Atlanta*, by Rodney T. Cohen (Arcadia).

9/29/03: *Black Enterprise: Titans of the B.E. 100s: Black CEOs who Redefined and Conquered American Business*, by Derek T. Dingle (John Wiley & Sons, Inc.).

10/6/03: *Their Eyes Were Watching God*, by Zora Neale Hurston (HarperCollins Publishers Inc.).

10/13/03: "What Happened to Your Generation's Promise of 'Love and Revolution'?: A Letter to Angela Davis" by Eisa Nefertari Ulen. First published in *Letters of Intent: Women Cross the Generations to Talk About Family, Work, Sex, Love, and the Future of Feminism* (The Free Press).

10/20/03: *The Best of Simple*, by Langston Hughes (Hill and Wang).

10/27/03: *The Rose That Grew from Concrete*, by Tupac Shakur (MTV Books/ Pocket Books).

11/3/03: *By the Work of Their Hands: Studies in Afro-American Folklife*, by John Michael Vlach (University Press of Virginia).

11/10/03: *Bloods: An Oral History of the Vietnam War by Black Veterans*, by Wallace Terry (Ballantine Books).

11/17/03: *Basic Black: Home Training for Modern Times*, Karen Grigsby Bates and Karen Elyse Hudson, (Bantam Doubleday Dell Publishing Group, Inc.).

12/1/03: *Black Women in America: An Historical Encyclopedia: Volume II*, edited by Darlene Clark Hine, Elsa Barkley Brown, Rosalyn Terborg-Penn (Indiana University Press).

12/8/03: *Christmas Soul: African American Holiday Stories*, as told to Allison Samuels, with paintings by Michele Wood (Jump at the Sun, Hyperion Books for Children).

12/15/03: *The African American Holiday of Kwanzaa: A Celebration of Family, Community and Culture*, by Maulana Karenga (University of Sankore Press).

12/29/03: "Lift Every Voice and Sing," by James Weldon Johnson was written in 1900 for a presentation in celebration of the birthday of Abraham Lincoln.